Contents

"Intelligence is the ability to adapt to change."

— Stephen Hawking

1. Paving Pathways to Enhanced Cognition

As our world races toward a future defined by innovation and technological advancement, the possibilities of enhancing human cognition and memory through structured techniques become not only fascinating but essential. Welcome to "Memory Palaces of the Future," a journey that explores the ground-breaking methods and intriguing theories shaping our understanding of memory and intelligence augmentation. In this book, we delve into a blend of ancient mnemonic techniques and cutting-edge cognitive sciences, creating a bridge where modern science meets age-old wisdom.

Imagine walking through a palace of your own design, where each room holds secrets to the information you wish to retain, every corridor echoing with the knowledge of your choosing. More than a metaphor, these memory palaces represent a practical framework for storing and recalling information with unprecedented clarity and speed. This book aims to equip you with the tools not just to imagine but to manifest such palaces as potent vectors for personal and intellectual growth.

Join me as we navigate the complex yet incredibly rewarding terrain of cognitive enhancement. This introductory chapter sets the stage for the expansive journey ahead, promising revelations that are often as inspiring as they are practical. So, are you ready to unlock the true potential of your mind? The future of your memory awaits.

2. The Origins of Memory Palaces

2.1. Ancient Mnemonic Techniques

Memory has long been a subject of fascination for philosophers, scholars, and practitioners, tracing a narrative that intertwines the winds of time and the evolution of human thought. Ancient mnemonic techniques represent some of the earliest methodologies developed to optimize memory and enhance cognitive performance. These techniques were not merely tools of retention; they were transformative approaches that allowed orators, scholars, and everyday individuals to navigate vast oceans of information, offering a glimpse into the cognitive framework that enabled the ancients to instill knowledge within a structured, memorable context.

The roots of mnemonic devices can be found in the intellectual traditions of ancient Greece and Rome, where the art of rhetoric was vital for public speaking, debate, and persuasion. The ability to remember and convey arguments was essential for success in civic life. Prominent figures such as Cicero and Aristotle documented various mnemonic strategies, emphasizing the importance of visualization and spatial orientation. These mnemonic strategies were designed to aid memory by creating associations with familiar places, images, and stories.

One of the most influential mnemonic techniques emerging from this period is known as the Method of Loci, or the memory palace technique, wherein individuals would mentally associate pieces of information with specific physical locations in familiar settings—their own homes or spaces they could visualize. This technique revolved around the principle that human memory is spatially encoded, allowing individuals to retrieve information by mentally 'walking' through a designated space where the information was anchored through vivid imagery. Practitioners would imagine placing pieces of information in particular rooms, aligning them with distinct sensory experiences that would cue their recall.

This process illustrated a profound understanding of the cognitive interplay between the mapping of memory and the nature of associative learning. Memory, it was discovered, is not merely about rote memorization; it blossoms when individuals engage with the material in meaningful, imaginative ways. Associated imagery, both familiar and abstract, have historically enriched the mnemonic experience, allowing for deeper embedding of knowledge within the human mind.

Another equally important aspect of ancient mnemonic techniques was their emphasis on narrative. The Greeks and Romans commonly utilized storytelling as a means of embedding information into memory. By transforming data into a storyline—complete with characters, conflict, and resolution—practitioners were able to enhance their retention and recall. Epic poetry and oral traditions thrived through this form of mnemonic structuring, revealing the intrinsic connection between memory and narrative.

In addition to the Method of Loci, ancient scholars developed a range of mnemonic rhymes, acronyms, and symbols as mnemonic devices. These techniques created mental shortcuts that simplified the encoding process and provided easier retrieval methods. By projecting information into rhyme or song, elements of rhythm and melody helped facilitate the memorization of complex ideas or lengthy facts. The clever use of alliteration, assonance, and other linguistic devices made information memorable and accessible, shaping a foundation that influenced not only ancient scholars but also later developments in educational practices.

Culturally, mnemonic practices were adaptive and transformative, spreading beyond the confines of Greek and Roman civilizations. Different societies leveraged these ancient techniques according to their linguistic, cultural, and educational contexts. In India, ancient practitioners utilized similar methods in the context of Vedic chanting, where memorization of extensive texts was facilitated through rhythmic recitation. In the Middle Ages, mnemonic devices permeated through the works of scholars who sought to preserve ancient wisdom while integrating it into their own theological and philosophical texts. This interleaving of memory and culture underscored the universal relevance and applicability of mnemonic techniques across time and geography.

As we evolved into the Renaissance and beyond, these techniques became further refined with advancements in educational philosophy and cognitive science. Notably, with the advent of printing, the landscape of memory techniques began to shift. As texts became more accessible, the necessity for rigorous memorization lessened; however, the cognitive principles established by these ancient techniques remained integral to our understanding of memory and learning.

Thus, the ancient mnemonic techniques laid down a foundational framework for memory enhancement that resonates even today. The mnemonic palaces envisioned by ancient orators were not merely physical spaces but represented a cognitive architecture that aligns closely with contemporary understandings of memory retention, neuropsychology, and cognitive science. These techniques demonstrate the timelessness of certain cognitive principles: that by engaging the imagination, harnessing spatial awareness, and framing information through narrative and association, we can significantly elevate our capacity for learning and recall.

As we stand on the cusp of a new era, where cognitive augmentation is being integrated with cutting-edge technology, an exploration of these ancient techniques becomes increasingly relevant. We find ourselves at a unique intersection where age-old wisdom converges with modern needs, encouraging us not just to remember but to comprehend and innovate, merging the capabilities of our minds with the tools of the future. Embracing these techniques is not merely a journey back into history but a proactive engagement with the cognitive abilities that define our humanity, igniting passion for learning and discovery that can last a lifetime. This significant legacy, rooted deeply in our cognitive history, invites us to build upon it, crafting memory palaces that extend into the natural and digital worlds—thus ensuring that the art of remembrance evolves alongside human progress.

2.2. The Method of Loci: A Historical Perspective

The Method of Loci, often referred to as the memory palace technique, boasts a rich historical tapestry that weaves together the innovations of ancient civilizations and the modern cognitive sciences. To understand its profound impact on memory enhancement, we must traverse its evolution from its ancient origins to its contemporary applications.

The inception of the Method of Loci is tied inextricably to the intellectual currents of ancient Greece, primarily attributed to the teachings of Simonides of Ceos, a renowned poet and thinker. The legend goes that Simonides, after witnessing a tragic collapse of a banquet hall, was able to identify victims merely by visualizing where they had been seated, illustrating the direct connection between spatial memory and recall. This incident not only highlighted the power of spatial awareness but laid the groundwork for a structured mnemonic method that would endure through the ages.

As the Method of Loci developed, it found a staunch ally in rhetoric —a discipline celebrated for its emphasis on memory as a means of persuasion and communication. Rhetoricians recognized that effective public speaking necessitated the retention of vast amounts of information, which led to an increased reliance on visual and spatial techniques. Thus, the Loci method became intertwined with the art of persuasion, transforming how orators structured their speeches and arguments. This technique hinged on creating mental maps that allowed speakers to place different points or arguments along a familiar route, thereby facilitating a smooth and memorable delivery.

In the Roman era, scholars like Cicero and Varro elucidated the Method of Loci, incorporating it into their writings on rhetoric and memory. Cicero articulated the idea that one could 'walk' through a physical space in their mind, retrieving information nestled within various loci—specific locations that served as memory cues. This metaphor of walking through a memory palace became the cornerstone of this mnemonically rich technique. It illustrated the profound understanding that human cognition relies on spatial structures, allowing individuals to retrieve encoded information more effectively.

The passage of time saw the Method of Loci adapting to cultural shifts while retaining its core principles. During the Middle Ages, the resurgence of interest in classical learning reinvigorated the Method of Loci, especially within monastic traditions. Monks utilized spatial mnemonic techniques to memorize extensive religious texts and scriptures, ensuring the preservation of knowledge amidst turbulent societal changes. In this context, the method acted not merely as a tool for memorization but as a vehicle for spiritual engagement and theological exploration, proving its adaptability to contrasting cultural narratives.

The Renaissance period marked yet another transformative phase for the Method of Loci. As humanism blossomed, scholars sought to reconcile classical knowledge with emerging scientific and artistic inquiries. Treatises written by figures like Giovanni Battista Della Porta celebrated the method's utility in education and artistic expression. This led to an era where mnemonics were employed not just for rote learning but as a means of enhancing creativity and imaginative thinking. The interplay between memory techniques and the burgeoning emphasis on individual intellect defined an age where knowledge was viewed through a more humanistic lens.

However, with the advent of the printing press, the pressure to memorize diminished significantly. Knowledge became marred in books rather than being retained mentally, leading to a decline in the emphasis on memory techniques such as the Method of Loci. The proliferation of printed material reshaped how knowledge was consumed, gradually detaching culture from mnemonic practices. Yet the principles underpinning the Method of Loci remained potent, laying dormant within the tapestry of educational philosophy and cognitive studies waiting for resurgence.

As we transitioned into the 20th and 21st centuries, the Method of Loci experienced a revival, propelled by renewed interests in cognitive science and neuroscience. The dawning understanding of the brain's neurological underpinnings and how memory functions at the physiological level brought fresh lifestyles and applications to ancient techniques. Modern cognitive theories espoused the significance of visualization and emotional engagement as pivotal components of memory retention—a foundation that resonated with the ethos of the Method of Loci.

Contemporary applications of the Method of Loci have transcended traditional environments and found fertile ground in a variety of domains—from educational tools for students to professional memory training in corporate settings. With the advent of technology, especially digital platforms, creating a memory palace is no longer confined to the confines of spatial imagination; it can extend into virtual realms, allowing individuals to mantle their mnemonic structures in dynamic ways.

Today, tools such as mobile apps and software that incorporate spatial memory techniques reflect a synthesis of ancient wisdom with modern technological advancements. These digital innovations offer customizable options for users to build intricate memory palaces that align with their personal learning styles, emphasizing the timeless relevance and versatility of the original concept. Artists, musicians, programmers, and professionals across diverse fields are embracing this enhanced approach to memory, highlighting the enduring connection between spatial orientation and cognitive retention.

In summary, the Method of Loci offers a fascinating lens through which to view the historical evolution of memory techniques. From its mythological origins in ancient Greece to its sophisticated manifestations in the modern age, the journey encapsulates humanity's quest to unravel the mysteries of memory. As we continue to reshape our understanding through ongoing exploration in neuroscience and cognitive science, the memory palace stands as both an emblem of historical significance and a beacon of future possibilities in the realm of intelligence augmentation. By grasping the elegance of this technique, we not only celebrate our cognitive heritage but foster an environment where enhanced memory and learning can flourish in an ever-evolving landscape.

2.3. Cultural Interpretations and Uses

Cultural interpretations and uses of memory techniques reveal a rich tapestry of human creativity, adaptability, and the perpetual quest for knowledge retention across civilizations. While the Method of Loci and other mnemonic techniques originated in ancient Greece and Rome, the adaptability of these methods in various cultural contexts showcases the universality of memory enhancement practices, demonstrating that the core principles of cognition transcend geographical and temporal boundaries.

In the context of Chinese culture, memory techniques such as storytelling can be intimately intertwined with the oral traditions that date back thousands of years. The Chinese tradition of storytelling —particularly the epic tales in texts like "The Book of Songs" or the historical accounts in "Records of the Grand Historian"—utilizes vivid imagery and structured narratives to educate listeners and ensure the transmission of cultural values. These centuries-old practices can be seen as a precursor to modern mnemonic devices, where the combination of visuals, emotions, and narratives creates strong memory hooks. The Chinese also have developed their own unique mnemonics, frequently relating to the Chinese characters' structures or meanings, allowing practitioners to anchor complex information to something visually and conceptually relevant.

In India, the interplay between memory and spirituality takes a profound form through Vedic chanting. Ancient scholars utilized rhythm, melody, and repetition to memorize extensive texts that formed the foundation of Hindu philosophy and spirituality. The practice of "Shruti," listening and remembering, combined with "Mantra," which utilizes specific syllables and sounds, creates a mnemonic environment that enhances cognitive retention while embedding spiritual significance within the memorized content. This holistic approach to memory—rooted in tradition, culture, and religious practice—exemplifies how communities can shape mnemonic strategies that serve multiple societal and spiritual purposes.

Moving across the world to the indigenous cultures of North America, we find similar principles at work in their oral histories and storytelling practices. Many Native American cultures emphasize the importance of memory through communal storytelling, where elders impart wisdom and cultural narratives that are stored collectively in the minds of the community. This cultural framework highlights the mnemonic value of stories that serve not only as entertainment but as a vital means of preserving identity, moral teachings, and historical events. The presence of visual markers—like landmarks in the landscape—often serves as mnemonic aids, creating a tangible connection between memory, place, and cultural identity.

In ancient Egypt, memory techniques were intricately tied to the creation of hieroglyphics, where symbols preserved vast amounts of knowledge. The "Book of the Dead," containing spells for the afterlife, relied on the memorization of complex symbols that were both visual and narrative in form. Egyptian priests employed various memory methodologies to ensure that these rituals were transmitted accurately across generations, showcasing an early form of structured mnemonic practices that drew from a combination of visual memory aids and oral recitation.

In contrast, the European Renaissance brought about a resurgence of interest in classical knowledge and the formalization of mnemonic systems once more. The likes of Giordano Bruno and other scholars proposed intricate systems that combined geometry, visualization methods, and complex layering of abstract concepts. Bruno's approach, known as "the art of memory," incorporated a blend of visual representations layered with symbolic meaning, unveiling the cognitive possibilities inherent in spatial and narrative memory techniques. This era's cultural rebirth reflected humanity's continuous engagement with enhancing cognitive capacity through both art and science.

Moreover, the integration of memory devices into education has seen varied interpretations across cultures. In some African communities, proverbs and folktales are employed to teach lessons, moral values, and historical narratives, showcasing how memory techniques are interwoven with the fabric of social education. The societal emphasis on memory not only strengthens individual recall abilities but also fosters a sense of community as shared narratives forge connections among individuals.

The rapid advancement of technology has further catalyzed the evolution of memory techniques across cultures in the modern era. Many cultures are embracing digital tools that retain the fundamental principles of ancient practices while responding to contemporary information overload. Social media, online learning platforms, and digital storytelling have transformed how histories and narratives are communicated and memorized, bridging cultural divides and creating global communities informed by diverse memory practices.

As we explore cultural interpretations and uses of memory techniques, we uncover the essential human drive to remember, learn, and share knowledge. From Vedic chants in ancient India to storytelling in indigenous cultures, the adaptations of the Method of Loci and mnemonic strategies illustrate the rich variability of human thought and creativity. Each culture, while distinctive in its practices, shares a common goal of enhancing memory and preserving the wisdom that shapes its identity, ensuring that the legacy of remembrance endures while evolving to meet the challenges of the present and future.

The implications of these cultural adaptations are profound; they remind us that memory techniques are not monolithic but instead reflect the diversity of human experience and expression. Understanding how different cultures interpret and utilize memory enhancement methods unlocks insights into the cognitive functions that are universally applicable while respecting the unique contexts in which these practices arise. As we stand on the brink of an era in which cognitive enhancement via technology intersects with age-old wisdom, we can look to these rich cultural narratives to guide our innovations, ensuring a holistic and inclusive approach to memory and learning.

2.4. Forgotten Memories: Revival of an Art

The resurgence of ancient memory techniques in modern times is an exhilarating reflection of humanity's persistent quest for cognitive enhancement. Forgotten for centuries as the advent of the printing press altered the landscape of knowledge retention, these monumental techniques have witnessed a revival, now interwoven with contemporary scientific understanding and technological advancements. This revival is not merely a nostalgic glance at the past; it is a dynamic, innovative synthesis of historic practices with modern cognitive frameworks, offering not only a deeper appreciation of our intellectual heritage but also practical tools for enhancing our cognitive capabilities today.

Just as the ancients constructed intricate memory palaces within their minds, modern practitioners are beginning to reestablish these mnemonic structures, recognizing their power in the age of information overload. The revival is marked by a diverse array of memory-enhancing strategies, which from a broad perspective can be identified as a multi-faceted effort to reclaim the efficacy of these techniques while adapting them to contemporary lifestyles. Inspired by both cognitive science and the need for increased efficiency in information retention, this movement showcases an awakening to the power of our cognitive architecture.

Prominent among those rediscovering these practices are educators, psychologists, and memory athletes who recognize the utility of ancient mnemonic methods like the Method of Loci. In various educational environments, both formal and informal, memory palaces have started to take center stage. Teachers are leveraging these memory techniques to enhance learning outcomes, promoting methods that encourage students to create personal memory frameworks where they can 'walk' through their learning materials. This approach paves the way for deeper understanding and retention of intricate subjects, encouraging students to interactively engage with their content in vivid, imaginative ways.

A significant aspect of this revival involves technology. As the digital age blossoms, the marriage of ancient techniques and contemporary tools has birthed personalized memory applications. Apps that allow users to build their own memory palaces—integrating visual aids and interactive experiences—have gained traction among individuals seeking to optimize their recall abilities. This dynamic application of ancient techniques resonates powerfully, as it embodies a harmonious blend of historical wisdom and innovative technology. The convenience of smartphones and dedicated memory software creates tools that not only facilitate memory retention but also make learning engaging and fun.

Recognizing the efficacy of emotional engagement in memory retention, modern practitioners have also brought forward new strategies that build emotional connections alongside ancient mnemonic methods. These techniques extend beyond rote memorization, embracing storytelling, visualization, and even gamification. By weaving emotional narratives into the learning experience, practitioners tap into a deeply-rooted aspect of human cognition that enhances recall. Moreover, this eclectic approach draws significantly from psychological research, underscoring the importance of emotion in the memory formation process.

The winds of change in how we perceive memory training are further supported by neuroscience's groundbreaking discoveries. An understanding of neuroplasticity—the brain's capacity to form and reorganize synaptic connections—has propelled forward initiatives aimed at enhancing cognitive abilities. These insights dovetail beautifully with the revival of ancient memory techniques, as they provide the foundational understanding that memory can be trained, shaped, and improved. Practitioners are now equipped with the scientific backing to implement and promote memory enhancement methods that embrace both ancient wisdom and contemporary cognitive theories.

Across the globe, this renaissance of memory practices finds its foothold within rehabilitative contexts, aiding individuals with memory challenges or cognitive decline. Therapies employing structured mnemonic techniques have showcased their impact in clinical settings, not only aiding recovery but also improving the quality of life for those experiencing memory-related difficulties. The mindfulness approach inherent in these techniques contributes positively to mental health, fostering not merely memory enhancement but overall cognitive well-being.

This revival extends beyond the confines of academic and clinical realms; it is permeating popular culture. Media outlets, books, and self-improvement programs showcasing these ancient techniques have proliferated, raising public awareness about the potential of memory enhancement. Public interest in memory competitions and the impressive feats exhibited by memory champions further spotlight the relevance of these practices in fostering an understanding of the mind's capabilities. This growing curiosity invites a new generation to engage in exploration and practice of memory techniques.

As we witness the renaissance of these forgotten arts, it becomes apparent that the revival of memory techniques reflects a broader societal need. In an era marked by rapid technological advancement and overwhelming information influx, the pursuit of cognitive enhancement has transformed from a niche interest into a vital necessity. Memory techniques serve as a bridge linking past knowledge to future innovations, and their revival signals a collective acknowledgment that our cognitive heritage is not just an echo of history but an asset poised to bolster our collective intellectual capacity.

In summary, the rediscovery of these monumental techniques marks a significant chapter in cognitive enhancement history. As both individuals and communities embrace the seamless integration of ancient practices with contemporary tools and theories, we foster an enriching dialogue between our past, present, and future. Memory has perhaps never been more essential, and in rediscovering how to harness it effectively, we unlock pathways to greater understanding, innovation, and communal connection. The revival of an art form that guided the orators of antiquity now empowers learners, educators, and global citizens alike—ushering in a new era where memory is not merely about retention but a mastery of an art that touches the very essence of our cognitive potential.

2.5. Foundations of Memory Architecture

A comprehensive understanding of memory architecture unveils how memory palaces function effectively as cognitive enhancement tools. At its core, memory architecture refers to the structural elements and principles that organize the ways in which we encode, store, and retrieve information. By exploring these foundational components, we can appreciate how the design of memory palaces catalyzes the process of memory recall, transforming the abstract concept of memory into a tangible and structured experience.

The first building block of memory architecture is the concept of spatial memory. Research indicates that human cognition is inherently spatial, with our brains wired to navigate and remember physical spaces. This intrinsic ability finds expression in techniques like the Method of Loci, wherein information is encoded based on its association with specific spatial locations, or "loci." Memory palaces leverage this aspect of our cognition by utilizing familiar environments where information can be anchored to particular locations, enhancing retention and recall. Spatial memory taps into our affinity for visual and environmental cues, thus enriching the mnemonic experience through associative learning.

Another critical aspect of memory architecture is the organization of information, which refers to the systematic arrangement of material into categories or hierarchies that facilitate processing and retrieval. The concept of chunking comes into play here, where large volumes of information are broken down into manageable segments that are easier to retain. Memory palaces employ this organizational technique by allowing individuals to group related information within distinct rooms or corridors of the palace, creating a mental structure that enhances the ability to retrieve related pieces of information simultaneously. This method not only simplifies the memorization

process but also aligns with the brain's natural propensity for catego-
rizing information.

In parallel with spatial organization, the principle of visualization
plays an essential role in memory architecture. Human memory is
inherently visual, responding better to vivid images compared to
abstract concepts. Memory palaces capitalize on this by prompting
users to create imaginative, sensory-rich visual representations of
the information they wish to remember. For instance, an individual
designing a memory palace might visualize a vibrant red apple for
the word "apple," placing it deliberately in a specific location within
the palace. This visualization links the abstract concept to a concrete
image, enabling more robust neural encoding and longer retention.
Thus, combining visualization techniques with spatial organization
entails creating a multi-sensory experience that significantly boosts
memory performance.

Additionally, emotional engagement within memory architecture
serves as a powerful augmenting factor. The emotional state during
the encoding process has been shown to influence memory retention.
Individuals tend to remember emotionally charged events better than
those that are neutral. Memory palaces can incorporate emotional elements by allowing users to create vivid, imaginative scenarios around
the information being encoded—this can involve weaving personal
experiences or impactful stories into the fabric of the memory palace.
Such immersive experiences enhance the emotional quality of the
memories, leading to deeper encoding and retrieval potential.

Moreover, narrative weaving within the architecture of memory plays
a crucial role. Building a coherent narrative around the information
allows individuals to interconnect disparate pieces of information in a
meaningful way. Memory palaces can serve as the backdrop for storytelling, whereby information is encased in a memorable sequence
of events, characters, and plots. A narrative framework transforms
isolated facts into an engaging story, promoting deeper understanding and recall. The fundamental human affinity for storytelling can

be strategically harnessed to bolster memory retention, making information more compelling and thus, more easily accessible.

On a physiological level, the neuroanatomy of memory formation aligns with the architecture of memory palaces. The hippocampus —the part of the brain involved in spatial navigation and memory —is particularly engaged when recalling information tied to specific physical locations. When individuals mentally traverse their memory palaces, they activate neural pathways linked to these locations, thereby facilitating recall. By understanding this connection, it can be appreciated that the design of a memory palace does not merely serve a psychological function; it is intricately tied to our brain's physiological underpinnings and capabilities.

Additionally, the interconnection between different types of memory —declarative (explicit) and non-declarative (implicit)—is relevant to memory palaces. Declarative memory involves the conscious recall of facts and events, which is directly engaged through structured memory methods. Conversely, non-declarative memory, associated with skills and procedural knowledge, can also be enhanced through techniques like memory palaces, suggesting that structuring information in this way can support learning across various types of memory. Reflective practices in memory architecture can harmonize these distinct forms of recall, creating a more comprehensive cognitive enhancement experience.

Finally, the adaptability of memory architecture must be recognized as a pivotal element. Memory palaces are not static; they can evolve with individual needs and learning objectives. This flexibility allows for personalized memory structures that cater to unique cognitive styles, preferences, and the types of information being retained. By regularly modifying and augmenting one's memory palace—adjusting rooms, adding items, or reformulating relationships between pieces of information—individuals can continuously refine their memory architecture, making it a living entity that grows alongside them. This adaptability ingrains resilience in the memory system, preparing it to absorb and retain new information effectively.

In concluding our exploration of memory architecture, it becomes evident that these foundational components collectively contribute to the potency and effectiveness of memory palaces. By integrating spatial awareness, visualization, emotional engagement, narrative weaving, physiological understanding, diverse memory types, and adaptability, memory palaces stand as a sophisticated framework designed for cognitive enhancement. As we delve deeper into the realm of cognitive sciences and memory augmentation, the insights gleaned from this exploration provide invaluable guidance for optimizing personal learning experiences and unlocking the potential of human memory. With memory architectures firmly established, the journey into memory palaces evolves into a promising avenue for personal growth, intellectual advancement, and a profound understanding of how we remember.

3. Cognitive Sciences and Memory Augmentation

3.1. An Introduction to Cognitive Science

Cognitive science is an interdisciplinary field that seeks to understand the nature of thought, learning, and memory through the integration of psychology, neuroscience, computer science, linguistics, philosophy, anthropology, and education. As we navigate an increasingly complex world, the relevance of cognitive science shapes our understanding of how humans process information, make decisions, and enhance their cognitive abilities. In this context, the exploration of memory takes center stage, particularly within the realm of cognitive enhancement and methodologies such as memory palaces.

At the heart of cognitive science lies the understanding that cognition encompasses a wide array of mental processes, including perception, attention, reasoning, problem-solving, and memory. Memory, as one of the cardinal components of cognition, is essential for learning and personal development. Through the lens of cognitive science, memory is not merely a passive storage system; rather, it is a dynamic process, scrutinized deeply to investigate how information is encoded, organized, stored, and ultimately retrieved.

The integration of cognitive science into the study of memory reveals crucial insights into the mechanisms involved in these processes. For instance, research in this field has uncovered two primary types of memory: declarative (or explicit) memory, which pertains to facts and events that can be consciously recalled, and non-declarative (or implicit) memory, encompassing skills and conditioned responses that are often performed unconsciously. Understanding these distinctions is instrumental in tailoring memory enhancement techniques to the individual, recognizing that different strategies may be necessary depending on the type of information being processed or retained.

Neuroscience contributes significantly to cognitive science by illuminating the biological substrates of memory. The intricate interplay between neurons, neurotransmitters, and brain structures, such as the hippocampus and amygdala, sheds light on memory formation and recall. As research techniques advance, from imaging technologies like fMRI and PET scans to electrophysiology, scientists have begun to map specific memories to particular neural pathways. This knowledge pushes the boundaries of memory enhancement by offering an empirical foundation for developing new methodologies, such as memory palaces, that can aid in optimizing cognitive function.

The cognitive load theory also plays a vital role within the cognitive science framework, highlighting the limitations of working memory and the implications of overloading cognitive resources. By understanding the capacity of working memory, we can create structured learning environments and mnemonic devices—such as memory palaces—that efficiently route information for better retention. In this way, cognitive science equips us with the principles necessary to design learning experiences that accommodate human cognitive limitations while maximizing understanding and memory enhancement.

With the rapid acceleration of technological advancements, cognitive science is increasingly intersecting with artificial intelligence and machine learning, leading to new perspectives on human cognition and memory augmentation. Cognitive models inspired by AI are being employed to simulate human memory processes, thereby allowing for the exploration of strategies that could assist in enhancing human memory. This relationship raises fascinating questions about the potential for collaborative human-AI partnerships in cognitive enhancement, as well as ethical considerations surrounding the impact of technology on our understanding of memory and cognition.

Moreover, the implications of cognitive science extend into practical realms, where the insights gleaned from research inform applications in education, therapy, and performance optimization. Cognitive science emphasizes the significance of tailoring learning strategies to align with the cognitive profiles of individuals, fostering an environment where memory retention can thrive. As such, educators and psychologists can utilize concepts from cognitive science to develop innovative teaching methods and techniques, further reinforcing the importance of memory within the broader tapestry of learning.

In summary, the exploration of cognitive science serves as a vital cornerstone in our understanding of memory and cognitive enhancement. By investigating the underlying processes of memory through multidisciplinary lenses, cognitive science not only enriches our comprehension of human cognition but also lays the groundwork for practical applications that empower individuals to harness their cognitive potential. This foundation paves the way for a future where structured methodologies and innovative technologies come together, enhancing memory and intelligence, and ultimately transforming the landscape of human learning and development. As we proceed in this book, we will further examine the neural underpinnings of memory, delve into the role of neuroplasticity, and explore how these scientific insights can be harnessed to create effective, personalized memory enhancement strategies.

3.2. Neural Foundations of Memory

Memory serves as one of the most intricate and dynamic functions of the human brain, encompassing a series of complex processes that allow us to encode, store, and retrieve information. To grasp the essence of memory at the physiological level, one must delve into the neural underpinnings that orchestrate this multifaceted phenomenon. At the core of memory formation are neurons—specialized cells that transmit electrical signals throughout the brain and body. These neurons are the fundamental building blocks of the nervous system, and their active communication is vital for all cognitive functions, particularly memory.

Memory can be broadly categorized into different types, the most fundamental being explicit (declarative) memory and implicit (non-declarative) memory. Explicit memory can be further divided into episodic memory, which pertains to personal experiences and specific events, and semantic memory, which relates to facts and general knowledge. Implicit memory encompasses skills and conditioned responses developed through practice or repetition. Understanding how these types of memory are processed requires a closer look at what happens in the brain during memory formation.

Encoding—an essential stage of memory processing—occurs when sensory information is transformed into a form that can be stored. The hippocampus, located within the temporal lobe, plays a crucial role in this phase. It acts as a gateway for new information, facilitating the transition from short-term memory to long-term memory. During encoding, the hippocampus interacts with various regions of the brain, including sensory areas and prefrontal regions, which contribute to higher-order cognitive functions such as attention and working memory. This interplay ensures that information is associated with relevant sensory experiences and contextual cues, enhancing the likelihood of successful retrieval later on.

Once encoded, information is consolidated, a process that transforms fragile short-term memories into more stable long-term memories. Consolidation primarily occurs during sleep and involves the strengthening of neural connections known as synapses. Repeated activation of specific neural pathways leads to structural changes in the brain, reinforcing synaptic connections—a phenomenon known as synaptic plasticity. The mechanisms of synaptic plasticity are heavily influenced by neurotransmitters, such as glutamate, which facilitate communication between neurons. Repeated activation results in long-lasting changes, commonly referred to as long-term potentiation (LTP), which plays a fundamental role in learning and memory.

The retrieval of memories—the process through which stored information is accessed—depends heavily on the cues present at the time of recall. This is where the associative nature of memory comes into play. The brain utilizes various cues, such as sensory inputs or contextual information, to trigger the activation of neural networks associated with a specific memory. Regions such as the cortex, which contains consolidated memories, work in tandem with the hippocampus to facilitate this retrieval process. Moreover, the emotional significance attached to certain memories, often processed by the amygdala, can enhance retrieval efficiency. Emotionally charged memories tend to be more vivid and easier to recall, shedding light on the interplay between emotion and memory.

Neurotransmitters also play a significant role in memory processes. Apart from glutamate, other neurotransmitters such as dopamine and acetylcholine are crucial for modulating memory functions. Dopamine is particularly important when it comes to reward-based learning; it reinforces the connections between neurons when an action leads to a positive outcome, thus enhancing the encoding of those memories. Acetylcholine, meanwhile, is linked to attention and arousal, supporting the encoding of new memories and facilitating memory retrieval.

As we investigate the neural foundations of memory, it is also pertinent to recognize that memory is not static; it is adaptive and malleable. The concept of neuroplasticity—the brain's ability to reorganize itself functionally and structurally in response to learning and experience—plays an essential role here. Neuroplasticity allows for the formation of new neural connections, the rearrangement of existing pathways, and the ability to recover from injuries. In the context of memory, this means that experiences can refine and reshape our memory systems, enabling us to learn more effectively and to adapt to new environments.

Furthermore, the brain's capacity for neuroplasticity can be harnessed through deliberate practice and mnemonic techniques, including those explored in the realm of memory palaces. By creating structured environments in the mind, individuals can facilitate the encoding and retrieval of information in a more organized and effective manner. Thus, memory palaces not only serve as vivid mnemonic aids but also take advantage of the brain's inherent adaptability, promoting an enduring capacity for memory enhancement.

In conclusion, exploring the neural foundations of memory reveals the intricate and interconnected processes that underpin how we learn, remember, and recall. Memory is not merely a passive archive of experiences; it is a dynamic interplay of various brain regions, neurotransmitters, and synaptic activities, all supported by the overarching phenomena of neuroplasticity. As our understanding of memory at the physiological level deepens, the implications for cognitive enhancement strategies grow clearer. Techniques such as memory palaces actively engage these neural mechanisms, allowing individuals to leverage their brain's natural capabilities for improved memory performance, ultimately transforming the way we approach learning and retention in an increasingly complex world.

3.3. Connections Between Mind and Memory

The connection between mind and memory is a profound avenue of exploration in cognitive enhancement, shedding light on how cognitive processes shape the ways we retain, recall, and utilize information. Understanding this relationship unveils the intricate mechanisms by which our minds manage the vast landscape of memories, revealing the interplay between thought, emotion, and cognition that influences memory retention and retrieval.

At its essence, memory serves as a repository of experiences and knowledge, the framework through which we navigate the world. It is not merely about holding onto information; memory is an active process that reflects our mental and emotional states. Our mind's ability to encode, store, and retrieve memories is closely tied to the cognitive processes we engage in—an interplay that underscores the significance of attention, association, and context in memory formation.

One of the key aspects of this connection lies in the concept of attention. The mind's capacity to focus on specific stimuli significantly impacts what information is encoded into memory. Cognitive psychologists have long recognized the importance of selective attention, whereby the brain filters through a torrent of sensory information, prioritizing what is deemed relevant or interesting. This principle demonstrates that our mental focus can shape our memory landscape, determining which experiences are transformed into lasting recollections. Without attention, memories are less likely to form; moments that lack cognitive engagement often fade away into obscurity.

Once information has been attended to, the next stage is the encoding process. This transformation of sensory experiences into a format usable by the brain is where the mind begins its work. Our experiences are not stored as isolated facts; instead, they are intricately woven into a tapestry of context, emotions, and prior knowledge. The mind acts as an architect, building connections and associations that will later serve as retrieval cues. For instance, if you study for an exam while in a particular location, the context of that space might become a vital cue that aids recall when you are in a similar environment during the test. Memories become more accessible when we leverage environmental cues and the associations we mentally construct.

The emotional aspect of memory cannot be overstated. Experiences laden with emotion are often the most vivid and easily recalled. Emotions can act as powerful enhancers of memory, shaping which details are remembered and which are forgotten. The interplay between emotion and memory is facilitated by the amygdala, a brain structure that processes emotional responses. When an event carries significant emotional weight—be it joy, sadness, or fear—the encoding process is heightened, ensuring these experiences have a prominent place in our memory bank. This phenomenon is evident in the way people often vividly recall where they were or what they were doing during moments of considerable emotional resonance, such as historical events or personal milestones.

The mind's ability to weave narratives also plays an instrumental role in connecting memory and cognition. Humans are inherently storytelling beings; narrating experiences engages cognitive processes that enhance memory. When we frame learned information as part of a story, we create a memorable context through which the data can be more readily accessed. Narratives draw on existing knowledge frameworks, fostering connections between new information and previously stored memories. This storytelling not only makes the material more relatable but reinforces our cognitive investment in the material, enhancing retention and recall.

As we delve deeper into the connections between mind and memory, it is crucial to recognize how cognitive frameworks can shape practices for memory enhancement. For instance, understanding the link between attention and memory can inform strategies such as mindfulness or focused learning sessions, which hone our ability to engage with information deeply. Techniques like spaced repetition and retrieval practice leverage cognitive principles to fortify memory retention by strategically structuring our encounters with information over time, solidifying pathways for efficient recall.

Moreover, emerging cognitive science research continues to highlight the importance of mind mapping and relational learning, techniques that capitalize on the associative nature of memory and its ties to cognitive processing. By employing visual diagrams or conceptual maps, individuals can create concrete representations of their knowledge, facilitating a clearer organizational structure for information retrieval. This interplay between visual and cognitive engagement illustrates how interconnected our mental processes are with memory.

As we look to the future of cognitive enhancement, recognizing the dynamic relationship between mind and memory opens doors to innovative approaches in education, mental health, and personal development. Insights into this connection encourage the development of tailored mnemonic strategies that encompass emotional engagement, personalized narratives, and nuanced cognitive frameworks. In this manner, we see memory not as a static function, but as a fluid and adaptable process—one that can be trained, cultivated, and optimized through conscious engagement and innovative techniques.

Ultimately, the connection between mind and memory is a testament to the intricate, multifaceted nature of human cognition. By understanding and harnessing these connections, we not only deepen our awareness of how we remember but also empower ourselves to construct memory palaces and cognitive frameworks that facilitate a more enriched, engaged, and informed experience of the world around us. The exploration of this connection marks a significant step in the quest for intelligent augmentation, as we seek to unlock the vast potential within our cognitive capabilities, bridging the ancient wisdom of mnemonic techniques with the burgeoning potential of cognitive science and technology.

3.4. Role of Neuroplasticity in Memory Enhancement

Neuroplasticity, the brain's remarkable ability to reorganize itself by forming new neural connections throughout life, plays a critical role in memory enhancement. This fundamental property of the brain allows it to adapt in response to experiences, learning, and environmental changes. Our understanding of neuroplasticity has expanded significantly in recent years, revealing that it is not just a mechanism for recovery after injury, but also a vital component in learning and memory formation. When we engage in memory enhancement techniques, such as building memory palaces or employing mnemonic devices, we actively harness the power of neuroplasticity to strengthen memory function.

At the neurobiological level, memory consolidation involves a series of processes that can alter the synaptic strength and structure of neural networks. When we remember something or learn a new fact, the brain encodes that information by creating a pattern of activity that affects the synaptic connections between neurons. Specifically, the hippocampus plays a pivotal role in the formation of new memories by facilitating the encoding process. Once information is encoded, it is subsequently consolidated into long-term memory, a process that benefits from neuroplastic changes.

Neuroplasticity can be viewed through two main processes: synaptic plasticity and structural plasticity. Synaptic plasticity refers to the ability of synapses—connections between neurons—to strengthen or weaken over time. Long-term potentiation (LTP) is one critical example of synaptic plasticity; it occurs when repeated stimulation of a synapse results in an increase in synaptic strength, enhancing the ability to transmit signals between neurons. This process is essential for learning and is particularly vital when engaging in memory techniques. When using the Method of Loci, for instance, as individuals mentally traverse their memory palaces, the act of retrieval and the associated visual and spatial cues activate specific neural pathways, thereby reinforcing the connections involved in memory recall.

Structural plasticity, on the other hand, pertains to the brain's ability to physically change its structure by forming new neural connections. This is particularly important in the context of learning and memory, as experiences can lead to changes in the number and arrangement of synapses. Engaging in memory-enhancing practices stimulates these structural changes, reinforcing the networks that support memory storage and retrieval. As individuals practice memory techniques, they are essentially training their brains to create and maintain these connections, resulting in improved recall capabilities.

The implications of neuroplasticity extend far beyond mere memory retention; they encompass cognitive flexibility, skill acquisition, and even emotional regulation. By embracing memory-enhancing techniques, individuals can foster an environment conducive to neuroplastic changes that positively impact their overall cognitive function. Brain-training practices, such as mindfulness, physical exercise, and deliberate cognitive challenges, can also serve to bolster neuroplasticity, creating a feedback loop that enhances memory performance over time.

Moreover, emerging research indicates that neuroplasticity is influenced by various factors, including age, lifestyle, and environmental enrichment. While neuroplasticity is most pronounced during critical developmental periods, adults demonstrate a substantial capacity for plastic change. This affirms the potential for lifelong learning and memory enhancement, suggesting that age should not be seen as a barrier to cognitive improvement. It also emphasizes the importance of maintaining a healthy lifestyle—engaging in regular physical activity, balanced nutrition, social engagement, and mental stimulation can enhance neuroplasticity and, consequently, memory capacity.

In addition to lifestyle factors, the advent of technology provides new avenues for fostering neuroplasticity. Digital memory aids, interactive learning platforms, and virtual reality environments can incorporate principles of spatial memory and cognitive engagement, stimulating neuroplastic changes in real time. They offer innovative ways to reinforce learning experiences, allowing users to create personalized memory palaces that effectively leverage the brain's adaptive capabilities.

The interconnected relationship between neuroplasticity and memory enhancement complements the broader narrative of cognitive enhancement techniques and underscores the importance of adopting practical strategies to optimize cognitive function. By understanding the principles of neuroplasticity, individuals can embrace a growth mindset—recognizing that their brains are capable of evolving and adapting in response to their efforts, thereby reinforcing the connections that form the bedrock of memory.

In conclusion, the role of neuroplasticity in memory enhancement is pivotal and multifaceted. It illuminates the biological mechanisms that underpin our ability to learn, adapt, and improve cognitive function throughout life. Through deliberate practices, such as the use of memory palaces and other mnemonic techniques, individuals can leverage neuroplasticity to create lasting changes in their memory systems. As we continue to explore the intricacies of the brain's adaptive capabilities, it becomes increasingly clear that memory enhancement is not only a possibility but a profound reality that can transform the way we learn and engage with the world. By embracing this knowledge, we open ourselves to a future where the boundaries of memory can be pushed, expanded, and redefined.

3.5. The Promise of Cognitive Science in Everyday Life

In the tumultuous landscape of modern life, where the sheer volume of information can often feel overwhelming, the promise of cognitive science emerges as a beacon of hope for enhancing memory and cognitive function in our everyday experiences. The advancements in cognitive science hold immense potential for reshaping our understanding of memory, transforming not only academic pursuits but also personal, professional, and social dimensions of our lives. By harnessing insights from various disciplines within cognitive science, individuals can leverage evidence-based techniques to significantly enhance their memory capabilities.

One of the most striking real-world applications of cognitive science is the increasing recognition of structured mnemonic techniques, flipping the narrative around memory from being a passive vessel to an active, trainable faculty. These techniques, including the venerable Method of Loci or memory palace strategy, have been incorporated into educational systems, corporate training, and personal development programs, enhancing retention and recall in ways that resonate deeply in today's information-saturated environment.

Within academic settings, students have begun to adopt these memory-boosting techniques to optimize their learning and improve retention rates. The transformation is not merely theoretical; schools and universities that implement cognitive science principles, combined with memory techniques, report noticeable improvements in student performance and engagement. By utilizing memory palaces—metaphorical spaces where they can anchor and retrieve information—students experience increased confidence in their abilities to handle complex material. This method reflects an empowering shift in educational practices, where students are not just recipients of information but active participants in their cognitive development.

Furthermore, cognitive science principles meld seamlessly with contemporary workplace environments, addressing the modern-day challenges of cognitive overload and decreased productivity. Professionals are increasingly turning to structured memory techniques designed to optimize their learning trajectories, retain essential information, and enhance their critical thinking. Workshops and training programs incorporating cognitive science insights emphasize memory strategies as tools for better performance at work. Employees can utilize mnemonic devices to master new software, learn technical jargon, and navigate complex procedures with ease—a necessity for today's fast-paced corporate landscape.

The implications of enhancing memory through cognitive science extend beyond the realms of education and work; they seep into our social interactions as well. By cultivating stronger memories—underpinned by techniques rooted in cognitive science—individuals enhance their ability to forge meaningful connections, remember details about others, and engage more effectively in conversations. The reinforcement of these skills has a ripple effect on personal relationships, providing the tools needed to engage in richer dialogue and deepen bonds with friends, family, and colleagues alike.

Moreover, as cognitive scientists continue to unlock the intricacies of human memory, applications that integrate technology and neuro-science have begun to emerge. Virtual reality (VR) and augmented reality (AR) technologies offer immersive experiences that can help individuals create vivid memory palaces or practice memory techniques in engaging environments. These modern tools are partic-ularly unique because they combine cognitive principles with sensory experiences, allowing for enhanced retention and recall. Through carefully curated environments, learners can experience scenarios tied to their memory objectives, bridging the gap between knowledge and practical application.

Additionally, advances in artificial intelligence (AI) are paving new pathways for memory augmentation. AI tools are being developed to analyze individual learning patterns and preferences, customizing them to enhance memory. Such innovations pave the way for tailored interventions that address diverse cognitive needs, making memory enhancement accessible to a broader audience. By understanding an individual's educational background and learning style, AI can facilitate the design of highly personalized memory strategies that resonate with them, ensuring deeper engagement and more robust retention.

In the healthcare sector, the promise of cognitive science is further amplified. Memory training programs informed by cognitive theories are being employed in therapeutic settings, particularly for individuals facing cognitive decline or memory challenges. By integrating techniques that tap into neuroplasticity, healthcare professionals are witnessing the positive impacts of structured memory techniques on recovery and rehabilitation efforts. These interventions not only address cognitive deficits but also empower individuals to reclaim a sense of agency over their mental faculties.

In exploring cognitive science's role in our lives, the implications stretch far beyond individual memory enhancement. Communities, too, can benefit significantly from fostering memory skills and cognitive strategies. Strengthening communal memory practices—whether through participating in storytelling circles, attending workshops on mnemonic devices, or engaging in collaborative learning environments—can create a richer cultural fabric where knowledge is widely shared and retained.

Looking ahead, the trajectory of cognitive science promises to kindle a renaissance of memory-enhancing strategies that will intertwine with societal values, technological advancements, and evolving cultural practices. As we embrace the wisdom of cognitive science, the possibilities for innovation in memory augmentation are as boundless as human imagination itself. By standing at the intersection of ancient mnemonic techniques and modern scientific insight, we are poised to explore untold opportunities—transforming our approach to memory, learning, and ultimately, the future of human cognition.

Thus, as we journey into this dynamic realm where cognitive science meets practical memory application, we are not just witnessing a revolution; we are participating in the evolution of culture, education, and identity—a tapestry woven through the art and science of memory. This profound exploration offers profound implications for how we live, learn, work, and connect, illuminating a path toward a more knowledgeable and engaged society.

4. Building the Future: Modern Memory Palaces

4.1. Adapting Ancient Techniques through Technology

In the evolving landscape of cognition, the integration of ancient memory techniques with cutting-edge technology has opened up a plethora of possibilities for enhancing memory and cognitive abilities. As we seek to develop personalized memory solutions, it becomes essential to harness modern tools that augment and diversify these timeless mnemonic practices. This adaptation not only strives to preserve the essence of ancient wisdom but also magnifies it through the lens of contemporary innovation.

The foundation of adapting ancient techniques through technology lies in recognizing that technology can provide innovative ways to customize memory practices. One of the most prominent pathways has been the proliferation of digital platforms that allow individuals to create digital memory palaces. Using virtual environments, users can design and navigate 3D spaces that replicate the mental models historically used in memory palaces but adapt them to 21st-century learning styles. Imagine constructing a personalized virtual library or an expansive garden filled with items you wish to remember, each meticulously placed within a spatial framework designed to evoke rich sensory experiences.

Moreover, technological advancements enable individuals to tailor their mnemonic experiences further by incorporating multimedia elements. Traditional memory enhancements often relied on verbal or visual cues, but with technology, one can enrich memories through audio, video, and even interactive features. A user might, for example, associate a specific smell with a place in their digital memory palace, bridging sensory experiences that enhance recall. These immersive cues invigorate the recall process, allowing more profound recollection of information by engaging multiple senses simultaneously, thereby tapping into the brain's inherent neuroplasticity.

Another critical front in this intersection is the advent of mobile applications designed to facilitate memory enhancement. These apps offer various functionalities, ranging from visual prompts and spaced repetition algorithms to interactive quizzes and memory games. Users can create customized memory banks where they categorize information according to personal relevance or complexity, aligning with their academic, career, or personal goals. Such tools accommodate diverse learning styles, making memory practices more accessible to individuals regardless of their cognitive preferences. A student could utilize a memory app to quiz themselves on historical dates through flashcards, creating a personalized study experience that dynamically adapts to their learning curve.

Additionally, artificial intelligence plays a burgeoning role in the development of personalizing memory solutions. AI-driven applications can analyze individual learning patterns and present tailored strategies for memory enhancement. They can recommend specific types of mnemonic devices based on user performance, predict when memory is likely to falter, and suggest review periods. This not only allows for personalized learning experiences but also maximizes the effectiveness of memory interventions, making it possible to develop bespoke strategies that align with the user's specific cognitive profile.

A further benefit of technology in memory enhancement is the expansion of collaborative learning opportunities. Social interaction has long been recognized as a vital component of effective learning and memory retention. Online learning platforms that incorporate community-based features facilitate group memory practices where users can share insights, strategies, and personal memory palaces. This collaborative approach capitalizes on the diversity of experiences and knowledge within a collective, allowing a richer exchange of mnemonic techniques and enhancing the overall learning environment.

Moreover, integrating virtual reality (VR) with memory practices creates immersive experiences that allow users to engage with material in visceral ways. By simulating scenarios or environments where specific information is contextualized, VR can effectively boost memory retention by anchoring information within rich, simulated experiences. This technology mirrors the techniques of ancient mnemonic devices while creating modern platforms for cognitive enhancement.

The importance of data security and ethical considerations cannot be overlooked as we adapt these ancient techniques through technology. With the vast expansion of digital memory solutions, ensuring that users' data remains private and secure has become paramount. Ethical frameworks need to be developed to guide the use of AI and data analytics in memory augmentation, protecting users while fostering innovation.

As we approach the future of memory enhancement, the possibilities for integrating technology with mnemonic strategies appear limitless. Beyond digital memory palaces and interactive applications, the exploration of neural interfaces and brain-computer interactions promises to further redefine how we enhance memory and cognition. These advances could potentially lead to direct communication between the brain and devices designed to enhance recall capacity and facilitate information storage.

In summary, the adaptation of ancient techniques through technology holds immense promise for memory enhancement. By combining the wisdom of historical mnemonic methods with modern scientific advancements, we pave the way for personalized solutions that cater to modern needs while honoring the legacy of our cognitive heritage. The journey ahead invites us to explore, innovate, and integrate, unlocking boundless potential for enhancing memory and thus enriching learning in an increasingly complex world. As we delve deeper into this realm, we find that the future of memory is not only about retention but about creating meaningful connections between knowledge, context, and experience.

4.2. Virtual Reality and Memory Systems

As we navigate the terrain of cognitive enhancement, virtual reality emerges as a groundbreaking tool with extraordinary potential for enhancing memory systems. This intersection of technology and psychology creates immersive experiences that redefine how we encode, organize, and retrieve information. Utilizing virtual reality (VR) in memory training harnesses the brain's natural propensity for spatial learning, making it a powerful ally in enhancing memory retention.

At the heart of VR's impact on memory systems lies the creation of immersive environments that engage multiple senses while providing a platform for constructing memory palaces. Unlike traditional learning modalities, which may involve passive reception of information, VR places users in fully-realized, three-dimensional spaces. This enhanced sensory experience fosters deeper connections between information and spatial contexts, significantly affecting how memories are formed.

For instance, when individuals navigate a VR memory palace they have constructed, they are not just passively recalling facts; they are actively engaging with the information through the sensations of sight, sound, and even touch. This multisensory engagement is vital, as it aligns seamlessly with how our brains naturally learn. Research has shown that information presented in immersive environments is often remembered more effectively than that presented in conventional formats. By creating a vivid 'world' within which to engage with new information, VR taps into the brain's innate strengths, accommodating various learning styles and enhancing recall capabilities.

Additionally, VR allows for the dynamic placement of memories in virtual spaces, facilitating unique forms of organization. Unlike static lists or flashcards, virtual environments enable users to conceptualize and navigate their information spatially. Imagine walking through a virtual museum where each exhibit corresponds to a different subject you wish to remember, with the detailed context, imagery, and sounds enhancing the overall learning experience. This synthesis of learning and engagement merges mental imagery with physical action, reinforcing pathways that are engaged during the recall process.

One significant advantage of VR is its ability to create contextual richness. Context is a fundamental aspect of memory retention; when we learn something within a specific context, it's often easier to retrieve that information when in a similar environment. With VR, users can tailor these learning contexts to their preferences and needs, creating scenarios that resonate personally with them. This personalization creates an emotional connection, further solidifying the memory. For example, placing historical events in the very locations where they occurred can provide a deeper understanding and emotional engagement, solidifying facts in memory.

Furthermore, virtual reality also promotes active learning through gamification. By incorporating game-like elements into the learning experience, VR environments can motivate users to engage in repeated practice—a crucial factor in memory retention. Such engagement transforms tedious rote memorization into a compelling and enjoyable experience, making information more memorable. Users are far more likely to revisit and rehearse their memories in a virtual game format designed to test and strengthen their recall. This active involvement is critical, as frequent exposure and interaction are essential for the consolidation of memory.

The role of neuroplasticity further enhances the efficacy of VR in improving memory systems. As discussed, neuroplasticity allows for the formation and adaptation of neural pathways in response to learning experiences. Virtual reality can facilitate this process by providing frequent and immersive experiences that train the brain to strengthen its memory circuits. Each time a user engages with a VR environment, they stimulate the neural pathways associated with that knowledge. With continued practice, this results in increased synaptic connections, leading to more robust and enduring memories.

Moreover, the adaptability of VR in catering to individual learning preferences and needs marks its significance in personalized memory training. For instance, educators and trainers can use VR systems to design custom experiences that align with specific learning objectives or cognitive challenges faced by individuals. Whether creating environments suited for practicing public speaking, learning foreign languages in culturally-relevant settings, or navigating complex anatomical structures in medical education, VR offers an unparalleled degree of customization that caters to diverse learners.

While the potential is immense, the implementation of VR in memory enhancement also requires thoughtful consideration of accessibility and usability. As with any technology, barriers to access can hinder its widespread adoption. Ensuring that VR systems are user-friendly and financially accessible will be essential in encouraging broader use among learners, educators, and stakeholders in various fields, including healthcare, education, and corporate training.

In summary, virtual reality stands at the forefront of memory enhancement, providing immersive, engaging environments that significantly bolster the processes of memory encoding, storage, and recall. By engaging sensory experiences, promoting contextual richness, facilitating gamification, and leveraging the principles of neuroplasticity, VR establishes a dynamic platform for individuals to strengthen their memory systems. As this technology continues to evolve, it holds the promise of transforming learning experiences, creating compelling avenues for cognitive enhancement that will shape the learning landscape of the future. With its ability to mesh ancient mnemonic strategies with modern technological advancements, VR is well-poised to redefine how we approach the art and science of memory in an increasingly complex world.

4.3. Digital Mnemonics: Apps and Software

In the digital era, where information flows incessantly and attention spans often fall short, innovative tools are emerging to reshape the landscape of memory practices. Digital mnemonics—spanning apps and software—represent a marriage of ancient techniques with cutting-edge technology, transforming how individuals encode, store, and retrieve information. In the context of modern cognitive enhancement, these tools offer a plethora of strategies to optimize memory performance while inviting interactive and engaging user experiences.

The rise of digital mnemonics is marked by a variety of mobile and desktop applications designed to ease the burdens of memory recall. These platforms leverage principles of cognitive science to transform traditional mnemonic techniques into vibrant and dynamic interfaces. By creating visually appealing layouts and incorporating gamified systems, these applications attract users to engage with their memory-enhancing activities actively. One prominent aspect of these tools is the integration of the Method of Loci—often depicted as a mental journey through a meticulously designed space, such as a familiar home or a fantastical landscape—into the heart of digital applications. Users can build their memory palaces, anchoring pieces of information at specific locations and creating vivid mental images that enhance retention.

For many, the appeal of such applications lies in their adaptability and personalization. Each user can customize their memory palaces, shaping their learning experience according to their preferred modalities, interests, and cognitive styles. These applications often allow for the incorporation of multimedia elements—images, sounds, and texts—that cater to diverse sensory channels, ultimately enriching the memorization process. For instance, an individual studying a foreign language could pair vocabulary words with sound pronunciations and relevant images, resulting in a comprehensive and immersive approach to memory encoding.

Moreover, digital memory tools often incorporate spaced repetition algorithms, a phenomenon grounded in cognitive psychology that optimizes timing for information review. By intelligently scheduling revision sessions for specific items stored in a memory palace, these tools can lead to longer retention periods, effectively mitigating the forgetting curve. This approach empowers users to take control of their learning journeys, guiding them at intervals that capitalize on their cognitive performance patterns.

Additionally, digital mnemonics harness collective memory—user-generated content shared among communities. Applications that facilitate peer-to-peer relationships allow individuals to share mnemonic devices, learning strategies, and various memory enhancement techniques, fostering an ecosystem of collaborative learning. By tapping into diverse experiences and background knowledge, users can enrich their own learning journeys while developing a sense of camaraderie in the quest for improved memory performance.

Another transformative dimension lies in the integration of artificial intelligence (AI) and machine learning algorithms within these apps. AI can analyze an individual's learning patterns, tailoring the interface and memorization strategies to maximize efficiency and effectiveness. By understanding how users interact with information, AI-driven applications can suggest alternative mnemonic methods, highlight areas for improvement, and predict when memory recall may falter. This personalized feedback loop can create a guided and adaptive learning environment, making memory enhancement a truly customized experience.

Cognitive trainers and memory games have also gained traction in the realm of digital mnemonics. These applications employ cognitive load principles, offering challenges designed to boost working memory capacity and cognitive flexibility by integrating gameplay elements that promote active engagement. Users navigate puzzles, challenges, and memory feats that cultivate cognitive skills while instilling enjoyment in the learning process.

However, while the promise of digital mnemonics is vast, it is essential to approach these tools with consideration. Ensuring that users do not become overly reliant on technology for cognitive processes is paramount, as it could inadvertently diminish the intrinsic skills developed through manual memorization techniques. Balancing the convenience afforded by technology with the timeless benefits of traditional mnemonic strategies is crucial in this evolving landscape.

Furthermore, accessibility remains a critical concern. The proliferation of advanced apps must extend to diverse populations, ensuring that everyone can benefit from these innovative tools. As developers continue to enhance features and interfaces, it is essential for collaborative efforts to focus on inclusivity and equity, providing accessible memory resources across varying socioeconomic backgrounds.

In summary, the emergence of digital mnemonics represents a paradigm shift in memory enhancement practices. By integrating ancient mnemonic techniques with innovative findings from cognitive science and digital technology, users gain access to personalized, engaging, and effective memory strategies. These applications not only revitalize traditional methods, such as the Method of Loci, but also foster community collaboration, adapting to individual learning patterns in real-time. As we forge ahead in this digital era, it is crucial to embrace the possibilities these tools offer while maintaining an awareness of the core principles of effective memorization that have withstood the test of time. Through this synthesis of old and new, we stand poised to explore new frontiers in memory retention and cognitive enhancement.

4.4. Integration of AI with Human Cognition

The integration of artificial intelligence (AI) with human cognition marks a transformative shift in how we approach memory enhancement and cognitive function. This convergence of technology with human capabilities holds incredible potential not only for improving memory but also for augmenting overall intelligence, creating synergies that were unimaginable only a few decades ago. By leveraging AI, we can foster an environment wherein human cognitive processes are supported, enhanced, and potentially redefined, paving the way for a future of unprecedented cognitive augmentation.

One of the most profound implications of integrating AI with human cognition lies in personalized memory enhancement. Traditional memory techniques, while effective, often take a one-size-fits-all approach. However, AI has the capacity to analyze an individual's cognitive profile, learning preferences, and retrieval patterns through data-driven insights. This analysis enables the development of tailored memory strategies that resonate with the user, offering optimized pathways for encoding, storing, and recalling information. Imagine a scenario where an AI-driven application learns from your engagement patterns—recognizing which mnemonic techniques help you retain information best or identifying when you are likely to forget specific details—and proactively adjusts its recommendations or prompts accordingly.

Moreover, AI can facilitate the automation of spaced repetition, a widely recognized memory-enhancing technique that involves scheduling review sessions based on the forgetting curve. By utilizing algorithms that calculate the optimal timing for revisiting information, AI can help individuals retain crucial knowledge more efficiently. This technology not only enhances memory retention but also alleviates the cognitive burden associated with self-management, allowing users to focus on higher-order tasks and engagement with content.

Another exciting avenue of exploration within this integration involves the use of natural language processing (NLP) tools. These AI systems can analyze vast amounts of text, distilling key concepts, themes, and associations, and presenting them in a more digestible format. Such tools can aid learners in comprehending complex materials, enabling them to extract pertinent information efficiently. By summarizing information and illustrating connections, NLP tools unlock layers of learning that support better retention and understanding.

The use of AI-powered virtual environments represents a significant leap forward in memory training. By creating immersive scenarios where users can engage with content actively, these systems enable individuals to harness the principles of experiential learning. For example, in a virtual reality (VR) setting, users can be transported to different historical periods or geographical settings, interacting with scenarios tied to the facts they seek to remember. AI can enhance these environments by dynamically adjusting them based on user actions and preferences, thus maximizing engagement and memory encoding. Users are not merely passive observers; they actively construct knowledge through immersive experiences—effectively reinforcing memory.

Furthermore, AI systems can serve as cognitive aids, assisting in the retrieval of information through contextual prompts or cues. By maintaining a continuous contextual understanding of an individual's activities or interests, AI can interject timely reminders, securing critical details when they are most relevant. For example, in a professional context, an AI assistant could retrieve pertinent information about an upcoming meeting based on stored data and ongoing project developments, allowing individuals to remain focused and informed in real time.

Beyond memory enhancement, integrating AI with human cognition invites us to ponder the ethical implications of such technology. As we become increasingly reliant on AI systems for cognitive tasks, one must consider concerns surrounding cognitive offloading and the potential atrophy of independent memory skills. The balance between leveraging technology for assistance and maintaining our cognitive faculties must be carefully navigated. Ethical frameworks should be established to govern the use of AI in cognitive enhancement, ensuring that it complements rather than supplants our cognitive abilities.

In turn, the evolution of AI-based cognitive enhancement opens discussions about the role of human agency in learning. While AI can offer substantial support, the intrinsic motivation to engage with memory techniques remains paramount. Engagement is driven not just by the technology available but by the mindset of the user. Therefore, education about cognitive processes, the nuances of memory techniques, and self-directed learning should be emphasized alongside technological solutions to create a holistic approach to cognitive enhancement.

As we look toward the future, the integration of AI with human cognition represents a frontier ripe with possibilities. Not only can we revolutionize how we enhance memory, but we can also perceive intelligence as a spectrum of capabilities that can be nurtured, developed, and expanded through this technological partnership. The vision of a future where AI collaborates with the human mind to foster unparalleled cognitive potentials is not a distant fantasy; it is an emerging reality poised to reshape our understanding of intelligence and memory.

Through ongoing research, dialogue, and practical exploration, we can cultivate this integration responsibly and effectively, ensuring that it enriches our cognitive experiences rather than detracting from our inherent abilities. In this journey of discovery, we stand on the precipice of what may very well redefine the parameters of human cognition, memory, and intelligence, growing into enhanced versions of ourselves in ways that expand the horizons of knowledge and understanding.

4.5. Future Perspectives on Memory Techniques

The future of memory techniques stands at a fascinating crossroads defined by technological innovation, cognitive science advancements, and a deeper understanding of human psychology. As we step further into the twenty-first century, it becomes evident that memory augmentation will not just be about retaining information but about integrating these enhancements into the very fabric of daily life, learning, and professional development. In this landscape, we will explore increasingly sophisticated methods of enhancing memory that blend ancient wisdom with contemporary technologies, offering transformative approaches to cognitive improvement.

Foremost among these advancements is the emergence of personalized memory strategies, shaped by individual needs, preferences, and learning styles. As artificial intelligence (AI) continues to evolve, we will increasingly see AI-driven applications that analyze the unique cognitive profiles of users. These platforms could recommend tailored mnemonic techniques, adaptive learning paths, and spaced repetition schedules designed to maximize retention based on the distinct ways individuals encode and retrieve information. This personalization marks a significant evolution in how we approach learning and memory enhancement—no longer simply a one-size-fits-all model but a dynamic system where strategies evolve alongside the learner.

Moreover, the integration of immersive technologies like virtual and augmented reality (VR/AR) will revolutionize the way we build and navigate memory palaces. Envision entering a richly rendered virtual environment where you can engage multiple senses, interact with virtual objects representing information, and physically traverse spaces tied to your memories. Such immersive experiences not only enhance memorization through deeper contextual understanding but also leverage our brain's affinity for spatial learning, enabling more effective recall. These environments will allow for muscle memory in learning, fostering a confident approach to retention through experiential, rather than solely theoretical, knowledge.

The role of collaborative learning will also reshape future memory practices. By fostering community-based learning environments—whether in virtual spaces or physical contexts—individuals will gain access to diverse perspectives and mnemonic strategies. Collective memory practices could lead to richer learning experiences, where knowledge is co-created and refined through shared paths of exploration. Such engagement encourages not only retention but also deeper insights into material through discussion, debate, and mutual reinforcement.

In addition, the emergence of cognitive science research will continuously inform memory techniques, advancing our understanding of how memory works physiologically and psychologically. Research into neuroplasticity—the brain's ability to reorganize itself and form new neuronal connections—will provide invaluable insights into creating effective memory enhancement strategies. With ongoing exploration in neuroscience, we anticipate the development of methods designed to optimize this plasticity, offering exercises that actively promote memory strengthening and retention through meaningful engagement.

As memory techniques grow increasingly sophisticated, ethical considerations surrounding their application will also surface. The implications of memory augmentation technology raise questions about the balance between enhancement and authenticity—how we ensure that our cognitive capabilities are not artificially manipulated but enriched. Discourse on these matters, combined with inclusivity in access to cognitive tools, will be crucial as society grapples with the emerging paradigms of memory enhancement. Ensuring that these advancements cater to diverse populations while maintaining ethical standards will foster a responsible approach to cognitive enhancement.

Furthermore, we may see a progressive shift in educational approaches, integrating memory techniques seamlessly into curricula from early education onwards. Schools may adopt cognitive science principles as foundational elements of teaching and learning, prioritizing memory-enhancing methodologies across subjects. Students could become adept at constructing their own memory palaces as a natural extension of lessons, reinforcing engagement and retention throughout their educational journeys.

Lastly, as we move further into the realm of digital cognition, the potential for global collaboration around memory enhancement initiatives will expand. International partnerships could enable a sharing of ideas, methods, and research related to memory enhancement, promoting cross-cultural exchanges that enrich collective understanding of cognitive techniques. This collaborative spirit will help create a global intelligence, empowering individuals to take charge of their learning experiences while fostering a greater appreciation for the multifaceted nature of memory across cultures and contexts.

In summary, the future of memory techniques promises to be as rich and varied as the human experience itself. By embracing innovative technologies, advancing cognitive science, and maintaining ethical considerations, we stand on the brink of a new era in memory enhancement that transcends traditional boundaries. This future is not merely about recalling facts; it is about building resilient cognitive architectures that allow for creative exploration, critical thinking, and the transformative empowerment of individuals navigating an increasingly complex world. As we continue to unlock the mysteries of memory and intelligence, we will empower ourselves to not only remember better but to think more deeply, harnessing our cognitive potential to its fullest extent.

5. Psychology of Memory and Learning

5.1. Theories of Memory Retention

Contemporary psychological theories and models of memory retention provide a multifaceted understanding of how we process, store, and retrieve information. As we advance our comprehension of memory mechanisms, it becomes critical to explore various frameworks that explain these complex processes, integrating insights from cognitive psychology, neuropsychology, and behavioral sciences. This exploration highlights the dynamic interplay between different types of memory, the factors that influence retention, and the potential strategies for enhancing memory efficacy.

One prominent framework in memory research is the Multi-Store Model of Memory, proposed by Atkinson and Shiffrin in 1968. This model posits that memory consists of three distinct stores: the sensory register, short-term memory (STM), and long-term memory (LTM). The sensory register captures information from the environment, allowing it to be briefly retained as sensory memory. Information then moves to short-term memory through processes like attention and perception, where it is held temporarily for further processing. If the information is encoded effectively, it can transition to long-term memory, where it may remain for extended periods, potentially across a lifetime. This model emphasizes the importance of attention and rehearsal in managing the flow of information between these stores, reflecting a linear progression of memory retention.

Expanding on this, Baddeley and Hitch's Working Memory Model (1974) introduces a more nuanced understanding of short-term storage. This model illustrates that short-term memory is not merely a singular entity but comprises multiple components working simultaneously to manipulate information. The central executive serves as a control system, orchestrating the functions of the phonological loop (verbal information), the visuospatial sketchpad (visual and spatial information), and the episodic buffer (integrating information from various sources). This multifaceted approach allows for greater complexity in how we understand activities such as reasoning and language acquisition, demonstrating that memory is actively constructed rather than passively received.

A central component of memory retention is the role of encoding, which can be influenced by factors such as depth of processing and the use of meaningful associations. Craik and Lockhart's Levels of Processing Theory (1972) posits that memory retention is intrinsically linked to the depth at which information is processed: shallow processing, which focuses on superficial characteristics (such as physical appearance), leads to weaker retention compared to deep processing, which considers semantic meaning. This theory underscores the significance of engagement and the use of mnemonic devices or techniques—such as the Method of Loci—that promote deeper processing through mental imagery and spatial organization.

In addition to encoding strategies, the Encoding Specificity Principle, introduced by Tulving and Thomson in 1973, emphasizes the context in which memories are formed. This principle asserts that retrieval cues must match the encoding context to optimize recall. For instance, environmental cues present during learning—like location, odor, or emotional state—serve as vital triggers for later recovery of information, revealing how context-dependent memory influences retention and recollection. It reflects the integral connection between our experiences and the effective retrieval of information stored in long-term memory.

Emotions further complicate and enrich our understanding of memory. Theoretical frameworks, such as the Affective Tagging Model, suggest that emotions not only enhance memory consolidation but also serve to distinguish between memories based on their emotional significance. This means that emotional experiences are often remembered more vividly and accurately than neutral ones, highlighting the intricate link between emotion and memory retention. The amygdala plays a vital role in this process, modulating how emotional experiences are encoded and influencing the biological underpinnings of memory formation.

Cognitive load theory, developed by Sweller in the 1980s, also plays a critical role in understanding memory retention, particularly in educational contexts. This model posits that cognitive load—defined as the total amount of mental effort being used in working memory—can significantly impact the learning process. When cognitive load is appropriately managed, it allows for effective processing and retention of information. However, when learning tasks exceed cognitive capacity, memory retention can deteriorate, resulting in frustration and diminished learning. By breaking down information into manageable chunks and reducing extraneous cognitive load, educators can create optimal environments for memory retention.

Incorporating motivation into memory theories, the Self-Determination Theory (SDT) elucidates how intrinsic and extrinsic motivators influence memory processes. This theory posits that when individuals feel autonomous, competent, and connected to others, their intrinsic motivation increases, thereby enhancing learning and retention. When learners engage with material actively and meaningfully, intrinsic motivation enhances their cognitive commitment to encoding and retrieving information effectively, significantly improving memory outcomes.

Cognitive-behavioral techniques have also emerged as practical applications for enhancing memory. Incorporating principles from cognitive-behavioral therapy (CBT), these strategies encourage individuals to identify and alter negative thought patterns that interfere with memory performance. Techniques such as cognitive restructuring, mindfulness meditation, and visualization can empower learners to improve focus, reduce anxiety, and enhance memory retention.

Finally, considerations surrounding neuroscience applications in understanding memory retention encompass emerging discoveries regarding neural pathways and brain connectivity. Techniques like functional neuroimaging have allowed researchers to visualize and analyze the neural substrates of memory in real-time, enhancing our understanding of how memory is rendered biologically and the specific brain areas involved in encoding, consolidation, and retrieval.

In conclusion, contemporary theories of memory retention synthesize a diverse range of insights from psychology and neuroscience, creating a rich tapestry of understanding around how memory functions. By exploring models that elucidate encoding strategies, the emotional landscape of memory, cognitive load management, and the integration of motivational factors, we gain valuable tools for enhancing memory. These theories not only inform our approaches to education and learning but also offer practical frameworks for individuals seeking to augment their cognitive abilities. As we continue to advance our knowledge of memory processes, we pave the way for innovative strategies that can profoundly influence personal growth and intellectual success.

5.2. Memory: An Emotional Journey

Memory processes are profoundly intertwined with our emotions, creating a nuanced landscape where feelings significantly influence how we retain and retrieve information. This connection between memory and emotion has been a focal point of psychological research, revealing insights that can reshape approaches to learning, retention, and cognitive enhancement.

Emotions have a dual role in shaping memory. On one hand, they serve as critical catalysts for memory encoding, while on the other hand, they influence retrieval processes. The neural mechanisms behind this phenomenon mainly involve structures like the amygdala and hippocampus, which work in tandem to process and store emotional experiences.

When we encounter information or experiences that evoke strong emotions—be it joy, anger, fear, or sadness—our brains are more likely to encode this information into memory. Emotional events are typically remembered with greater clarity and longevity compared to neutral ones. This heightened recollection can be attributed to the amygdala's activation, which enhances the encoding of memories tied to intense emotional states. The memory of a traumatic event, for instance, can remain vividly etched in our minds, with details persisting over time due to the emotional weight carried by such experiences.

Similarly, joyful memories, such as celebrations or significant life milestones, are often recalled with vividness and detail because of the strong positive emotions associated with them.

Moreover, emotional memories can be subject to what's known as "flashbulb memory," a phenomenon where individuals can recall the specific details of an event that held significant emotional impact. The memories of where one was during a life-altering incident—like a historical event or a personal tragedy—illustrate how emotions can create lasting impressions that influence the ability to retrieve information later on. In this sense, emotions not only govern the learning process but also ensure that certain memories are more readily accessible because of their significance.

The role of emotions extends to retrieval as well. When we are in a similar emotional state as when we first encoded the memory—a concept known as "mood congruence"—we are more likely to recall related memories. For example, if someone is feeling nostalgic, they may more readily remember past experiences tied to happiness or sadness. This phenomenon may explain why certain songs or scents can evoke powerful memories; they can re-trigger an emotional context that facilitates recall.

In contrast, emotions can also serve as barriers to effective memory retrieval. For instance, feelings of anxiety or stress can hinder one's ability to access certain memories. This highlights how the emotional context—influenced by our current mental state—can either enhance or inhibit learning and recall. When individuals experience test anxiety, for example, their emotional state can cloud their memory retrieval, leading to underperformance in educational settings. Addressing emotional well-being, therefore, becomes critical for optimizing memory performance.

Understanding the emotional dimension of memory has significant implications for educational practices and training programs. By incorporating techniques that emphasize emotional engagement—such as storytelling, visualization, and creating relatable scenarios—

educators can foster stronger connections to the material, enhancing both retention and recall. For instance, rather than presenting facts in isolation, embedding them within a narrative or experiential context can create emotional resonance that solidifies learning.

Additionally, interventions aimed at developing emotional intelligence and resilience can further bolster memory processes. By equipping learners with skills to manage their emotions, they can minimize stress and anxiety, creating a conducive environment for memory encoding and retrieval. Furthermore, fostering a supportive and positive learning atmosphere can engage students' emotions in a constructive way, reinforcing their ability to retain and recall information effectively.

In summary, the interplay between memory and emotion reveals a rich framework shaping how we learn and remember. Emotions act as both facilitators and hindrances in memory processes, underscoring the importance of considering emotional contexts in cognitive enhancement strategies. By leveraging emotional engagement in educational settings and personal development, we can transform the landscape of memory enhancement. The marriage of memory and emotion thus emerges as a powerful ally in the quest for effective learning, paving the way for deeper understanding, retention, and fulfillment in both academic and personal pursuits.

5.3. Cognitive Load and Its Implications

Cognitive load is a critical concept in understanding how humans process information and the implications for memory enhancement. Cognitive load refers to the amount of mental effort being used in the working memory, which is inherently limited in capacity. This limitation necessitates a careful balance in how information is presented and processed, particularly when adopting strategies like memory palaces for learning and retention. The implications of cognitive load extend across educational practices, personal learning strategies, and even workplace training, underpinning how effectively information can be retained and recalled.

At the core of cognitive load theory is the recognition that our brains can handle only a finite amount of information at any given moment. When cognitive load exceeds the working memory's capacity, it can lead to cognitive overload, resulting in diminished learning, increased errors, and retention failures. This phenomenon is particularly relevant in settings where new information is presented alongside complex tasks, ultimately hindering effective memory encoding. In the context of using memory techniques, such as the Method of Loci or constructing memory palaces, paying attention to cognitive load becomes essential for optimizing learning outcomes.

There are three distinct types of cognitive load: intrinsic, extraneous, and germane. Intrinsic load refers to the inherent difficulty associated with a specific topic or task; it is dictated by the nature of the content itself and is influenced by the learner's existing knowledge and skill level. For instance, a student learning advanced calculus will experience a higher intrinsic load compared to one studying basic arithmetic, as the former entails more complex operations and concepts. This aspect emphasizes the importance of prior knowledge in shaping the efficacy of memory techniques—individuals who possess a solid foundation in relevant subjects will find it easier to assimilate and organize new information.

Extraneous load encompasses the cognitive demands placed on learners by the manner in which information is presented. This includes any unnecessary distractions that may divert attention or complicate understanding. For example, a cluttered presentation slide filled with excessive text and images can lead to cognitive overload, making it challenging for learners to focus on critical details. When utilizing memory techniques, it is vital to minimize extraneous load through clear, concise, and engaging presentations of information. Well-structured memory palaces should be free from irrelevant details that could hinder the recall process.

Germane load refers to the cognitive effort dedicated to processing and transferring information into long-term memory. This type of load promotes understanding and learning, focusing on meaningful engagement with the material. When employing memory techniques, effectively managing cognitive load encourages germane processing —facilitating the encoding of information within mental structures like memory palaces. Strategies such as breaking down complex information into manageable chunks, employing vivid imagery, and incorporating meaningful associations can help learners create lasting connections, thus enhancing retention through meaningful engagement.

The implications of cognitive load for memory enhancement are vast. In educational contexts, understanding cognitive load enables educators to design effective curricula that optimize learning. This can involve tailoring lesson content to align with students' existing knowledge, minimizing distractions, and integrating engaging learning strategies that foster involvement with the material. By strategically considering cognitive load, educators can enhance the overall effectiveness of memory techniques and promote deeper learning.

In professional environments, awareness of cognitive load can inform training programs that aim to enhance employee retention of new skills or information. During onboarding or professional development sessions, trainers can apply principles of cognitive load theory to structure content delivery effectively. This might involve using simulations or interactive activities that reinforce essential concepts without overwhelming employees with excessive information. By aligning training with cognitive principles, organizations can foster an environment conducive to effective learning and long-term retention.

Furthermore, individuals seeking to enhance their cognitive abilities can leverage cognitive load principles in their personal learning strategies. When building memory palaces, for example, one can prioritize intrinsic load by focusing on familiar or relevant subjects that align with their prior knowledge, allowing for a smoother encoding process. Strategies that minimize extraneous load, such as avoiding distractions and structuring information clearly, can create an optimal environment for memory enhancement. Additionally, fostering germane load through active engagement increases the likelihood of encoding the information effectively into long-term memory.

The intersection of cognitive load and memory techniques underscores the importance of tailored approaches in learning and memory enhancement. By balancing intrinsic, extraneous, and germane loads, educators, professionals, and learners alike can create structured environments for effective information retention. As cognitive load continues to be explored in research, incorporating this understanding into our everyday practices will enhance cognitive capabilities and cement the role of memory palaces as powerful tools for personal and intellectual growth. This model not only illuminates pathways to improved memory retention but also integrates seamlessly with the cognitive strategies outlined throughout this book. As we embrace these insights, we can confidently navigate the complexities of learning in a fast-paced, information-rich world, ensuring that the pursuit of knowledge remains rewarding and enriching.

5.4. Motivation and Memory Enhancement

Motivation plays a crucial role in enhancing memory retention and recall, impacting how effectively individuals can absorb, process, and retrieve information. As we explore the connections between motivation and memory enhancement, we see that both intrinsic and extrinsic motivators can significantly influence cognitive performance, shaping the ways in which we engage with learning and memory techniques.

Intrinsic motivation refers to the internal drive to engage in an activity for its own sake, as opposed to for some external reward. This form of motivation can be linked to personal interests, curiosity, and the desire for mastery or self-improvement. When learners are intrinsically motivated, they tend to exhibit greater persistence, deeper engagement, and more effective learning strategies. This enthusiasm enhances their ability to encode information into memory, as they are more likely to relate the material to their own experiences, aspirations, and emotional states.

Research in cognitive psychology has consistently shown that intrinsic motivation can lead to improved memory outcomes. For instance, studies have indicated that individuals who find personal relevance in the material they are studying demonstrate higher retention rates and better recall. Engaging with content that resonates personally often allows learners to devise their mnemonic techniques, such as creating meaningful visualizations or employing the Method of Loci. When learners forge emotional connections with the information, they enhance its memorability and accessibility.

Conversely, extrinsic motivation is driven by external factors, such as rewards, recognition, or grades. While extrinsic motivators can effectively prompt immediate engagement or compliance, their long-term impact on memory retention can vary. In some cases, external rewards might lead to superficial learning—where individuals focus solely on meeting the criteria for rewards without genuinely internalizing the material. This approach can hinder deeper cognitive processing, which is essential for transferring information into lasting memory. Therefore, while extrinsic motivators can kick-start engagement, they are often most effective when complemented by intrinsic motivation that fosters a genuine desire to learn and understand.

To leverage the benefits of motivation in memory enhancement, educational approaches should strive to cultivate intrinsic motivation by fostering an engaging and supportive environment. This can involve incorporating choice within the learning experience, allowing learners to select topics or areas of interest that align with their personal goals. Moreover, providing opportunities for self-directed learning can empower individuals to take control of their educational journeys, further fueling intrinsic motivation.

Goal-setting is another powerful strategy for enhancing motivation and memory retention. Establishing clear, achievable goals helps individuals to chart their path and build a sense of ownership over their learning process. As learners reach milestones, they experience a psychological boost that reinforces their motivation and encourages continued engagement with the material. This accomplishment not only heightens intrinsic motivation but also solidifies the connections in memory, as each goal achieved becomes an anchor for associated knowledge.

Furthermore, the incorporation of authentic, real-world applications can serve to enhance motivation by emphasizing the value and relevance of what is being learned. By showcasing how knowledge or skills can be applied contextually, learners are more likely to see the practical implications of their studies. The emotional resonance of connecting learning with real-life experiences reinforces memory by embedding it within meaningful frameworks.

As we delve deeper into cognitive science and educational practices, the integration of motivational techniques will continue to shape how we approach memory enhancement. By understanding the dual roles of intrinsic and extrinsic motivation, educators, trainers, and learners alike can develop strategies that elevate memory retention through engaged and meaningful learning experiences.

Incorporating regular feedback is also vital in sustaining motivation and enhancing memory. Constructive feedback reinforces a learner's connection to the material, clarifying expectations, and guiding them toward incremental improvements. Since motivation often fluctuates, timely reinforcement of effort can reignite enthusiasm and encourage persistence, facilitating the encoding process.

As we consider cognitive behavioral techniques (CBT) as auxiliary tools for enhancing motivation, an understanding of how thoughts and beliefs underpin emotional states reveals new avenues for memory enhancement. Cognitive restructuring, a core aspect of CBT, allows individuals to challenge negative beliefs that may be contributing to diminished motivation or memories. By reshaping these cognitive patterns, learners can cultivate a positive mindset that reinforces their capacity to engage with memory techniques effectively.

In summary, the relationship between motivation and memory enhancement forms an intricate web where emotional engagement, personal relevance, and goal-oriented learning converge. By fostering intrinsic motivation while effectively utilizing extrinsic motivators, we pave the way for practices that not only optimize memory retention but also enrich the overall learning experience. As we navigate the complexities of cognitive enhancement, it is imperative to cultivate environments that inspire curiosity, promote meaningful connections, and ultimately empower individuals on their cognitive journeys.

5.5. Cognitive Behavioral Techniques

Cognitive behavioral techniques (CBT) play a significant role in enhancing memory and cognitive functions by addressing the interplay between thoughts, emotions, and behaviors. The principles underlying CBT can be strategically utilized to optimize memory retention, improve recall abilities, and foster a healthy cognitive environment. The therapeutic framework of CBT emphasizes the importance of understanding and modifying unproductive thought patterns, which can in turn positively affect how memory is encoded and retrieved.

At the core of CBT is the recognition that our thoughts influence our emotions and behaviors. This triadic relationship highlights the potential to change cognitive patterns in ways that bolster memory retention. By identifying cognitive distortions—misconceptions about oneself or situations that can lead to anxiety, fear, or decreased motivation—individuals can learn to reframe their thought processes. For instance, a student struggling with exam anxiety may initially think, "I'll never remember everything," leading to increased stress and impaired performance. Through CBT techniques, this thought can be challenged and restructured to something more constructive, such as, "I have learned this material and can recall parts of it effectively."

This reframing process is crucial for promoting a positive attitude toward memory tasks, encouraging a productive mindset that can enhance retention and retrieval of information. Techniques such as cognitive restructuring, which involves identifying negative thoughts and replacing them with more realistic or positive ones, empower individuals to engage with material in a way that feels manageable and achievable. When learners approach memory techniques like the Method of Loci with a confident mindset, they are more likely to encode and retain information effectively.

Moreover, mindfulness practices, often integrated into CBT, have shown promising results in enhancing cognitive functions. By cultivating a present-focused awareness, individuals can improve their attention and concentration, which are essential for memory encoding. When a person practices mindfulness, they engage more fully with the material they are trying to learn, allowing for deeper processing. This heightened level of engagement can significantly enhance recall abilities, as memories formed while in a mindful state tend to be more robust.

Behavioral strategies from CBT can also be employed to establish effective study habits and routines. For example, breaking down study sessions into smaller, focused intervals—commonly referred to as the Pomodoro Technique—creates structured opportunities for concentrated effort. This approach minimizes the cognitive load during study sessions, making it easier to absorb and retain information. By setting specific goals for learning, individuals can monitor their progress and celebrate incremental achievements, reinforcing a sense of mastery and motivation.

In addition to modifying thought patterns and behaviors, CBT also emphasizes the importance of managing emotions. Memory is closely tied to emotional states, and high levels of anxiety or stress can hinder effective recall. Cognitive behavioral techniques involve developing coping strategies to manage these emotional responses. For instance, relaxation techniques and visualization exercises can help calm nerves before a test or presentation, leading to clearer thinking and improved memory retrieval. Such techniques create an optimal environment for memory function during high-pressure situations by reducing the interference caused by anxiety.

Another practical application of CBT in enhancing memory involves the use of self-monitoring techniques. By keeping a learning journal to track thoughts, behaviors, and emotional states during study sessions or while attempting to recall information, individuals can gain insight into patterns that either support or hinder their memory performance. This self-awareness can be a powerful tool for making necessary adjustments, such as identifying when distractions or negative thoughts are influencing memory recall.

Further, integrating these cognitive techniques into structured memory-building activities can also optimize learning. For example, associating emotionally charged personal experiences with new information can enhance retention. A learner might create a memory palace filled with meaningful stories from their life, weaving emotional narratives around the information they wish to remember. By embedding such memories within personal contexts, retrieval cues become stronger, and recall becomes easier, illustrating the potent fusion of CBT principles with mnemonic techniques.

In essence, cognitive behavioral techniques offer robust strategies for individuals aiming to enhance their memory and cognitive capacities. By addressing the cognitive patterns that influence memory retention, developing effective study and coping strategies, and promoting mindfulness and emotional regulation, CBT empowers learners to optimize their retention, recall, and engagement with information. As we continue to explore innovative avenues for cognitive enhancement, embracing the principles of CBT represents a vital step toward realizing our full cognitive potential. The integration of these techniques not only provides immediate benefits in memory performance but fosters a resilient mindset that can navigate the complexities of learning in an increasingly challenging world.

6. Neuroscience Breakthroughs and Implications

6.1. Unveiling the Complex Brain Networks

As our understanding of the human brain deepens, recent studies have begun to unveil the complex networks that underpin memory processes, providing critical insights that could reshape our approach to cognitive enhancement. Central to this investigation is the realization that memory is not merely housed in isolated regions of the brain but is instead a product of intricate, interconnected networks that collaborate to encode, store, and retrieve information. This intricate web of neural connections, often referred to as the "memory network," illuminates the pathways through which experiences are translated into memories, laying the groundwork for advancements in mnemonic techniques, memory augmentation, and personalized cognitive strategies.

At the forefront of neuroscience, neuroimaging techniques such as functional magnetic resonance imaging (fMRI) and positron emission tomography (PET) have enabled researchers to explore the activation patterns of various brain regions during memory tasks. These insights have revealed that the hippocampus, long recognized as playing a vital role in the formation of new memories, is intrinsically linked with other regions, including the prefrontal cortex, amygdala, and sensory areas of the cortex. This cooperation among diverse brain areas allows for a more nuanced understanding of memory, highlighting that effective recall may engage not only the hippocampus but also regions responsible for emotion, sensory perception, and decision-making.

One crucial discovery emerging from this research is the concept of "memory reconsolidation," the biological process through which memories are recalled and subsequently stored again as they are reorganized. This process reveals the dynamic nature of memory—rather than being static entities, memories are malleable and can be updated or modified based on new information, context, or emotional states. Understanding this phenomenon presents exciting possibilities for cognitive enhancement, as it implies that targeted interventions, such as cognitive-behavioral techniques or spaced repetition, can be strategically applied during the reconsolidation phase to strengthen retention or alter existing memories.

Further exploration of neurotransmitter systems also highlights the role of chemical messengers in memory processing. For instance, the neurotransmitter dopamine is associated not only with reward processing but also with the reinforcement of memory pathways. This implies that enhancing dopamine availability could improve memory encoding and retrieval, offering a potential avenue for pharmacological interventions aimed at supporting memory functions.

Emerging studies are also elucidating the role of sleep in memory consolidation, emphasizing that a substantial portion of memory processing occurs during different sleep stages. While we sleep, the brain enters a state of 'offline processing', where newly acquired information is integrated with existing knowledge, strengthening neural connections. The significance of this insight cannot be overstated, as it underscores the importance of sleep hygiene in memory retention and overall cognitive health. Harnessing this knowledge could lead to guided interventions that not only promote healthy sleeping patterns but also utilize techniques that optimize memory retention and recall by aligning learning activities with restorative sleep.

Additionally, recent findings indicate that environmental factors play a vital role in shaping and influencing memory networks. Contextual cues—such as the physical space in which learning occurs or emotional states at the time of information encoding—can create powerful associations that enhance recall. This reinforces the ancient techniques of the Method of Loci, where spatial memory is leveraged to anchor information within specific environments, facilitating mental 'walks' through associated memories. These insights suggest that memory palaces not only serve as mnemonic tools but also capitalize on the brain's inherent connectivity for optimal retrieval.

The implications of these discoveries extend beyond academic contexts; they hold promise for applications in various domains, including education, therapy, and everyday life. Understanding how our memories function as interconnected networks allows educators to tailor learning experiences that enhance retention through meaningful contextual engagement. For instance, experiential learning, which involves immersive, context-rich activities, can create powerful associations, thereby strengthening memory pathways and promoting deeper cognitive engagement.

In therapeutic settings, these insights could inform interventions for individuals facing memory-related challenges, such as those recovering from brain injuries or dealing with conditions like Alzheimer's disease. By utilizing knowledge of how memory networks operate and adapting therapeutic strategies that promote reconsolidation and leverage environmental cues, practitioners could facilitate more effective memory rehabilitation.

Furthermore, as we consider the integration of technology with cognitive enhancement, understanding the complex brain networks behind memory enables us to develop more sophisticated memory-assisting tools—ranging from memory-training apps that utilize contextual cues to implement virtual reality environments that mimic real-life settings for immersive learning experiences.

In conclusion, the endeavor to unveil the complex brain networks integral to memory processing reveals a rich and intricate landscape that has profound implications for enhancing memory and overall cognitive function. As researchers continue to explore the exciting frontiers of neuroscience, the insights gained from these studies promise to empower individuals with practical tools and strategies to optimize their cognitive capabilities. This understanding of the interconnected memory network not only illuminates pathways for effective memory retention but also sets the stage for innovative approaches that enrich our cognitive experiences, blending ancient mnemonic wisdom with modern scientific expansion for a future where human memory flourishes.

6.2. Memory Pathways: Discovering New Territories

As neuroscience continues to unveil the intricacies of memory function, emerging research reveals new pathways and mechanisms that shed light on how memories are formed, retained, and recalled. These discoveries not only expand our understanding of cognitive processes but also pave the way for advanced memory enhancement techniques and applications in everyday life. The advancements in neuroimaging technologies, such as functional magnetic resonance imaging (fMRI), have illuminated the brain regions involved in memory processing, revealing that memory is a dynamic interplay of complex neural networks rather than isolated brain activities.

Recent findings have shown that memory is not merely the product of individual synapses firing in isolation but involves coordinated activity across multiple brain regions. The hippocampus remains a central player in the process of memory formation, particularly in converting short-term memories into long-term ones. However, it now appears that other regions, including the prefrontal cortex, amygdala, and various sensory cortices, work in concert with the hippocampus. The prefrontal cortex is critical for higher-order functions such as decision-making and executive functioning, which are essential for organizing and integrating information before it is encoded into memory. Meanwhile, the amygdala is renowned for its role in emotional memory, signaling how feelings can enhance the encoding process, which is invaluable when considering the designs of memory palaces and other mnemonic strategies.

Discovering how these networks collaborate has significant implications for creating tailored memory enhancement interventions. For instance, leveraging emotional triggers in experiences can lead to improved retention of information. Educators and trainers might integrate emotionally charged content or storytelling techniques into their curricula, enhancing memory retention by activating the emotional centers alongside cognitive processing areas. This multifaceted approach to memory-building echoes the age-old mnemonic strategy of associating emotional stories or visuals with information to embed it in memory more effectively.

Neuroscientists are also investigating the concept of "memory reconsolidation," revealing that when we recall a memory, it becomes temporarily malleable before being re-stored in its modified form. This finding carries profound implications for therapeutic settings, allowing for interventions such as cognitive restructuring to reshape traumatic memories or enhance learning. Memory-enhancing techniques, including the Method of Loci, can be integrated into these moments of reconsolidation, potentially fortifying the memory while also updating or reframing its emotional context.

Moreover, the exploration of neuroplasticity—the brain's remarkable ability to rewire itself based on experiences—further emphasizes the potential for memory enhancement. By engaging in structured learning and memory techniques, individuals can facilitate neuroplastic changes that strengthen memory circuits. This transformative potential invites the incorporation of technologies such as virtual reality and augmented reality, which can provide immersive experiences that stimulate both cognitive engagement and emotional activation, ultimately reshaping memory pathways more effectively.

The implications of this understanding extend into various areas, including education, therapy, and even technology development. In educational contexts, harnessing these insights can lead to enriched curricula that promote deeper cognitive engagement and retention. In therapeutic contexts, utilizing methods informed by these discoveries can aid in memory rehabilitation, allowing practitioners to support individuals in overcoming cognitive challenges. Furthermore, the emergence of digital memory tools that employ these principles can create interactive learning environments tailored to individual cognitive profiles, enhancing accessibility and effectiveness.

As we delve into the future of cognitive enhancement, recognizing the promising avenues revealed by the exploration of memory pathways will empower individuals to optimize their learning experiences and bolster their memory capacities. By synthesizing these discoveries with established mnemonic techniques, we have the potential to craft powerful memory enhancement strategies that align with the brain's natural mechanisms.

In summary, the ongoing research into the complex networks involved in memory processing offers invaluable insights into how memories are formed, retained, and transformed. These discoveries not only enhance our understanding of cognition but also highlight the potential for creating innovative memory enhancement techniques. By activating emotional responses, fostering neuroplasticity, and integrating multi-modal experiences, we can unlock new territories in memory enhancement and ultimately enrich cognitive performance. The journey into the science of memory remains promising, beckoning exploration into ever-expanding realms of understanding that celebrate the capabilities of the human mind.

6.3. Neuroscientific Approaches to Augmentation

With the rapid advancement of technology and our understanding of the brain, neuroscientific approaches to augmentation are revolutionizing memory enhancement techniques. In this emerging field, neuroscientists explore the brain's complex networks and underlying mechanisms, aiming to develop methods that tap into the innate capabilities of human cognition.

At the core of these neuroscientific approaches is the concept of neuroplasticity, the brain's ability to reorganize itself by forming new neural connections throughout life. This property allows the brain to adapt in response to learning and environmental experiences. It is evident that by strategically engaging with memory techniques, individuals can promote neuroplastic changes, ultimately enhancing their memory capabilities. Researchers are investigating techniques that can facilitate this process, particularly through the use of mnemonic devices, such as the Method of Loci, which leverages spatial awareness to reinforce memory recall.

One key area of research involves the role of neurotransmitters and hormones in memory formation. For instance, studies have shown that dopamine, associated with reward processing, plays a critical role in strengthening memory pathways. This insight signifies that enhancing dopamine availability could potentially improve memory encoding and retrieval, providing a direction for pharmacological interventions designed to support cognitive function.

Moreover, emerging technologies like brain-computer interfaces (BCIs) hold significant promise for augmenting memory. These devices enable direct communication between the brain and external devices, allowing for novel methods to assist with memory encoding and retrieval. BCIs could facilitate real-time feedback and reinforcement of memory techniques, creating personalized cognitive augmentation solutions that adapt to individual learning patterns.

Another innovative direction involves the application of virtual and augmented reality. These immersive technologies offer environments where users can engage with content dynamically, making it easier to anchor information within context-rich scenarios. For instance, navigating a virtual memory palace becomes more than a theoretical concept; it transforms into an engaging experience that taps into the brain's natural spatial memory strengths. Such environments not only enhance retention but also tap into the emotional aspects of memory, potentially reinforcing the encoding processes by creating memorable experiences.

As with any technological advancement, ethical considerations remain paramount in the implementation of neuroscientific augmentation techniques. Ensuring equitable access and addressing concerns surrounding cognitive privacy and data security will be critical as these methods become more widespread. Engaging in interdisciplinary dialogue among neuroscientists, ethicists, educators, and policymakers will ensure that we navigate these challenges responsibly.

While the promise of neuroscientific approaches to memory augmentation is vast, the field is still evolving, and challenges remain in translating laboratory findings into practical applications. To maximize the potential of these techniques, ongoing research must focus on identifying the most effective methods, understanding variations in individual responses, and developing comprehensive training programs that incorporate these approaches into everyday learning experiences.

In conclusion, neuroscientific approaches to memory augmentation illuminate extraordinary avenues for enhancing cognitive capabilities. As we deepen our understanding of the brain's intricate networks and leverage technological advancements, we move closer to developing practical strategies that empower individuals to maximize their memory potential. By fostering a culture of innovation and ethical consideration, we stand at the brink of a new era in cognitive enhancement, transforming the landscape of human memory for generations to come.

6.4. Potential and Pitfalls of Memory Augmentation

As the quest for memory augmentation unfolds, delving into potential benefits and challenges reveals a complex interplay between technology, human cognition, and ethical considerations. The future of memory enhancement, while full of opportunity, brings forth a series of potential pitfalls that warrant careful examination.

On one hand, the advancements in cognitive enhancement techniques promise to revolutionize the way individuals acquire, retain, and recall information. Memory augmentation could provide unprecedented benefits in various domains—including education, professional development, and personal growth. For instance, students who leverage digital memory tools and mnemonic strategies may experience improved academic performance, as they enhance their capacity to retain complex information. Professionals may find similar advantages, as refined memory skills contribute to efficiency and productivity in the workplace. Similarly, individuals seeking to improve their cognitive capabilities can use memory palaces and other mnemonic devices to heighten their learning experience and boost their creativity.

Moreover, emerging technologies—such as artificial intelligence (AI), virtual reality (VR), and neural interfaces—open doors for tailored cognitive enhancement. These technologies promise individualized training experiences, wherein algorithms adapt to users' cognitive profiles, ensuring that memory augmentation strategies align with personal learning styles and efficacy. By personalizing the memory enhancement experience through immersive engagement and targeted reinforcement, these innovations have the potential to reshape our understanding of what is possible within the realm of memory.

However, alongside these promising opportunities lie significant ethical, psychological, and societal implications. The accessibility of memory enhancement technologies raises concerns about equity; as access becomes stratified, individuals with limited resources could face disparities in cognitive capabilities, leading to wider societal inequalities. If cognitive augmentation techniques are only available to a select few, the gulf between different segments of society may widen, intensifying existing disparities in educational and professional opportunities.

Moreover, the reliance on digital tools for memory enhancement could lead to unintended consequences. As individuals increasingly depend on technology to aid their memory, there lies the risk of cognitive offloading—where mental effort is transferred to external devices at the expense of developing intrinsic memory skills. If over-reliance on digital memory aids becomes prevalent, it may hinder the natural development of memory capabilities, ultimately resulting in decreased intrinsic motivation to learn and recall without technological assistance.

The issue of ethical consent further complicates the discussion of memory augmentation. As cognitive enhancements turn from speculative fiction to reality, key questions arise: Who is responsible for facilitating access to these tools? Are individuals fully informed regarding the implications of utilizing memory enhancement technologies? Researchers, policymakers, and technology developers must address these ethical considerations to ensure that cognitive enhancements promote equitable societal outcomes while respecting the autonomy and consent of individuals.

Additionally, the psychological implications of memory augmentation deserve careful attention. As individuals engage with memory-enhancing techniques, the potential to manipulate or alter emotional responses tied to memories raises concerns. The fluidity of memories, where reconsolidation may enable modifications, suggests a need for caution when intervening with emotional memories. This interplay between emotions and cognition carries weighty implications for therapeutic practices, as emotional experiences remain foundational to personal identity. However, while memory enhancement can offer therapeutic benefits, it may inadvertently contribute to ethical concerns surrounding trauma recovery, manipulation, and potential erasure of individuals' lived experiences.

Finally, there is a philosophical component to consider within the discourse of memory augmentation. The very nature of memory and its relation to identity, authenticity, and personal history raises profound questions about what it means to be human. As cognitive enhancements blur the lines between natural and technologically-assisted memory, the existential implications shift our perceptions of self, intelligence, and human potential. The philosophical debates surrounding cognitive enhancement technologies invite reflection on the essence of knowledge and the moral boundaries we navigate in pursuit of intellectual augmentation.

In summary, while the allure of memory augmentation paints a hopeful future, navigating the complex landscape requires a multi-dimensional approach that amalgamates technological innovation, ethical considerations, psychological implications, and philosophical discourse. As we embrace the advances in cognitive enhancement techniques, a collaborative effort among researchers, policymakers, and practitioners will be essential to ensure that the quest for memory augmentation enriches lives without compromising our values and integrity. By fostering a responsible approach to memory enhancement, we will usher in a future where cognitive capabilities are expanded, enriching human experiences while remaining mindful of the multifaceted implications tied to this profound journey into the depths of memory.

6.5. Neuroethics: Moral Considerations

As we tread into the ethereal intersection of neuroscience, technology, and ethics concerning memory enhancement, we encounter a plethora of moral considerations that surround the use of emerging cognitive enhancements. As memory augmentation technologies become increasingly embedded in our daily lives, they elicit profound ethical debates that merit close scrutiny. These discussions span a wide range of issues involving the depth of human cognition, equitable access to enhancement tools, personal autonomy, and the implications of manipulating memory itself.

One of the central themes in the neuroethics discourse on memory enhancement pertains to the authenticity of human experiences. The use of advanced technologies like neural implants or pharmacological agents designed to enhance memory raises pressing questions about the integrity of the memories being formed. If one were to rely on artificially enhanced memory retention, how would we define the authenticity of those experiences? Would memories logically retained with technological assistance carry the same weight as those formed through lived experiences? Such philosophical dilemmas delve into the heart of what it means to remember and the implications of technology on the human narrative. The potential for individuals to selectively enhance or suppress memories rearranges the essence of identity and personal history.

Equally significant is the consideration of equitable access to memory augmentation technologies. As these advancements promise to bolster cognitive function and enhance learning capabilities, there exists a potential risk of deepening existing societal inequalities. Access to cognitive enhancement tools may be limited to privileged populations, risking the creation of a cognitive divide that leaves marginalized groups further behind. In assessing the moral implications, it is paramount to advocate for comprehensive access that ensures all individuals—regardless of socioeconomic status—can benefit from the potential advantages these technologies offer. Strategies should be formulated to promote inclusivity in the development and distribution of memory enhancement resources, thus preserving the values of equity and justice within cognitive intervention contexts.

Moreover, privacy and autonomy emerge as crucial topics in the ethical landscape of cognitive enhancement. The incorporation of technology into personal memory management means that aspects of one's cognitive processes may be accessible to external parties —whether that be through data collection, artificial intelligence algorithms, or device monitoring. The potential for unauthorized access to personal memories or sensitive information presents a serious ethical concern. Safeguarding individual privacy while ensuring that autonomy remains intact poses a significant challenge. It is essential that policies are developed to protect users and establish clear boundaries regarding consent and data use.

The manipulation of memory also raises pivotal ethical questions regarding the potential for misuse. With advanced cognitive technologies, malicious actors may exploit memory augmentation mechanisms for coercive or harmful purposes. For instance, if memories can be erased or altered, who stands to gain from this capability? The specter of "memory hacking"—the unauthorized alteration or removal of personal memories—opens avenues for exploitation. As such, ethical frameworks must be established to clarify the permissible parameters for memory intervention and the right to mental integrity.

Furthermore, there exists a dimension of psychological and emotional fallout tied to the enhancement of memory. Memory serves not only as a repository of knowledge but also as an anchor for personal identity and emotional experiences. The implications of altering or removing memories can have unintended consequences, leading to a distortion of self-understanding and emotional connections. The potential for trauma resulting from compromised memories reinforces the need for a cautious approach that prioritizes mental welfare alongside enhancement from technological interventions.

As cognitive enhancement technologies evolve, the ethical principles guiding their application must remain adaptable and responsive to emerging developments. The discourse surrounding memory enhancement must encompass a broad spectrum of perspectives —scientific, ethical, cultural, and philosophical. Dialogues among neuroscientists, ethicists, policymakers, and the public are critical to defining the healthy boundaries within which these advancements can be harnessed for positive societal transformation.

In summary, the exploration of neuroethics in memory enhancements confronts us with vital moral considerations revolving around authenticity, equitable access, privacy, potential misuse, and emotional ramifications. As we move into this new frontier defined by cognitive augmentation, concerted efforts to engage in meaningful and inclusive discussions on these ethical challenges will be paramount. Embracing memory enhancement opportunities responsibly ensures that we navigate these transformative advancements while upholding the values of humanity, integrity, and justice at their core. The exploration into these moral considerations ultimately lays the groundwork for how we selectively enter an era where cognitive enhancement can serve as both a boon and a burden, fostering our growth while demanding our conscientious stewardship.

7. Practical Guide to Constructing Memory Palaces

7.1. Steps to Building Your Own Palace

To construct your own memory palace, start by identifying a space that is familiar and comfortable to you. This could be your current home, your childhood residence, or a place you visit often, such as a favorite park or café. The familiarity of this setting will make it easier for your mind to navigate and visualize different aspects of the palace.

Begin by visualizing the exterior of your chosen location and then mentally enter. Each room in your memory palace will serve as a distinct segment where information can be stored. As you map out your palace, consider the layout carefully. The more vivid and unique the details you associate with each room, the stronger the connections to the information you wish to remember.

Next, assign pieces of information to specific loci, or locations, within your palace. This could be a chair in the living room where you might place information about a historical figure, or the kitchen table for a list of groceries or concepts related to a project. Creating strong visual or sensory associations with the information can dramatically aid memorization. For instance, you could imagine the historical figure flamboyantly dressed and sitting at the chair, engaging in a conversation about their contributions.

As you begin to populate your memory palace, use the Method of Loci effectively by walking through your palace mentally. Imagine yourself moving through each room as you recall different pieces of information. To reinforce your mental journey, consider narrating a story that connects the information with the space, incorporating your senses beyond just sight—think about smells, sounds, or even emotions linked to each location.

Once you have laid the foundation, practice retrieving the information at regular intervals to strengthen your memory. Initially, you might visualize your memory palace and walk through it several times to reinforce the connections. Gradually, aim to bring to mind the information associated with each location even without visualizing the palace itself—this enhances recall over time.

To further fortify your palace, enhance it with distinct themes or personal touches that resonate with you. For example, if you love a particular color or music genre, incorporating these elements into your visualization can heighten emotional connections. This strengthens the associative pathways in your brain, making the information even easier to retrieve.

Avoid common pitfalls as you build your memory palace. Many people overload their memory palaces by trying to cram too much information into one place, leading to confusion. Keep each room dedicated to a single topic or theme. Additionally, ensure that your mental images are vivid, as abstract or vague imagery can diminish cognitive engagement.

By using specific methods to measure your progress, you can assess how effective your memory palace has been. Track the ease with which you can retrieve information over time and make modifications based on your experiences. Are there areas where you struggle? Consider rearranging or reassigning information to different rooms to optimize your memory structure.

Consistency is key. With practice and regular use, your memory palace will transform into a robust tool for enhancing your ability to retain and recall vast amounts of information. Ultimately, the memory palace is not just a repository of knowledge; it's a personal creation that reflects your unique way of interacting with information, facilitating cognitive growth and enriching your learning process.

Through this detailed and structured approach, constructing your own memory palace becomes an engaging and effective exercise, merging the art of memory with the science of cognition. By embracing both personal significance and creative visualization, you'll unlock the full potential of your memory, paving the way for enhanced learning outcomes across various facets of life—academic, professional, and beyond.

7.2. Establishing Effective Mental Structures

Establishing effective mental structures involves both the foundational principles and advanced techniques that support memory enhancement. At the heart of this endeavor is the recognition that the way we organize and conceptualize information greatly influences our ability to retain and recall it. The architecture of our mental frameworks plays a critical role in shaping our cognitive processes, making it vital to establish effective structures tailored to individual learning styles.

The first step in establishing these mental structures is to identify clear objectives for what you want to remember. Determining the purpose behind your memory work provides direction, serving as the guiding principle for the entire process. Whether you're studying for an important exam, learning a new language, or preparing for a presentation, clarity regarding your goals allows you to create a roadmap for your cognitive journey. This initial step can be further enhanced by listing the key concepts or pieces of information you want to master, creating a blueprint for the memory structures to follow.

Next, employing mnemonic devices like acronyms, rhymes, and visualization techniques can enhance the establishment of mental structures. These devices serve as cognitive scaffolding, helping to anchor information within our memory architecture. For instance, when constructing a memory palace, you can visualize specific rooms in your palace designated for particular subjects or topics. Aligning these concepts with vivid and unique imagery enhances the memorability of the information and creates a more connected network of associations. The use of striking imagery amplifies the emotional engagement with the content, reinforcing the connections and making retrieval easier.

As you begin to develop your memory palace or mental framework, consider the organizational patterns that resonate within your cognitive style. Some individuals may prefer hierarchical structures, where information is categorized and prioritized within a logical framework. Others might find that clustering related ideas or using thematic connections serves them better. Whichever approach you adopt, the goal is to create a structured entity that feels natural, allowing information to exist in harmony rather than disarray. Consistency across the mental structures you build also aids retrieval, as a well-defined framework minimizes confusion during recall.

Incorporating repetition into this process is essential. Cognitive science emphasizes the importance of spaced repetition for solidifying memory retention. When you revisit the information at progressively spaced intervals, the neural pathways associated with those memories become more robust. Using a consistent schedule, plan regular review sessions where you mentally traverse your established memory structures, reinforcing the connections you have built. This repetitive engagement capitalizes on the way the brain consolidates and strengthens memories over time.

Another key feature in establishing effective mental structures is adaptability. Just like modern architecture can be reconfigured to suit the needs of its occupants, your memory frameworks should be flexible and cater to evolving information and learning objectives. If something no longer serves your cognitive needs, don't hesitate to modify your mental palace or restructure your mnemonic associations. This adaptability not only ensures the relevance of what you are remembering but also encourages ongoing engagement with the material, keeping your cognitive pathways lively and dynamic.

Utilizing multimedia resources can further augment the effectiveness of your mental structures. When building a memory framework, consider drawing from various sources such as videos, diagrams, and interactive apps to create a rich tapestry of information. Engaging multiple senses during the encoding of memories reinforces the neural connections, leading to deeper comprehension and more effective recall.

Moreover, social interaction can serve as a powerful catalyst in establishing effective mental structures. Engaging in discussions with others about the information you wish to remember allows for the exploration of various perspectives and connections that you might not have previously considered. This collaborative approach reinforces your memory frameworks while providing opportunities for deeper insight and understanding.

In summary, establishing effective mental structures for memory retention is a multifaceted process that encompasses clarity of objectives, visualization techniques, organizational strategies, meaningful engagement, and adaptability. By actively constructing well-defined cognitive frameworks, incorporating mnemonic devices, and continually reinforcing these pathways through repetition and social engagement, individuals can enhance their memory abilities significantly. The journey towards effective mental structures is not only an intellectual endeavor; it is an expedition into the very essence of how we learn, remember, and connect with the world around us. As we continue to explore these techniques and practices, we open up avenues for expanded cognitive capabilities, ultimately enriching our intellectual lives and enhancing our interactions with knowledge.

7.3. Personalization and Creativity in Design

As the role of personalization and creativity becomes increasingly significant in the art of memory enhancement, the strategies we develop can be uniquely tailored to fit our individual cognitive profiles, learning styles, and preferred memory structures. Personalized designs ultimately lead to a more immersive and effective memory experience. Infusing personal elements into memory techniques not only makes the process of learning and retention enjoyable, but it also encourages deeper cognitive engagement, ultimately resulting in more robust recall.

The first step toward building a personalized memory palace begins by reflecting on your own preferences and experiences. Each memory palace should resonate with the individual constructing it, serving as a true extension of their identity. Start by selecting a meaningful location—this could be your childhood home, your current residence, or a place that holds sentimental value to you. Such familiarity provides an immediate sense of comfort and relevance, making it far easier to navigate and populate the space with mnemonic devices.

Once you've chosen your location, think creatively about how to enhance your memory palace with personal touches—details like favorite colors, objects, or symbols that evoke positive emotions. Imagine, for instance, decorating your virtual space with images that are significant to you, incorporating elements that trigger positive memories or feelings. If you have a passion for music, consider including musical notes or instruments that symbolize different ideas or concepts you aim to remember. This creative personalization deepens the emotional connection to the space and the information within it.

Next, consider using storytelling as a device for infusing your memory palace with a narrative structure that feels uniquely yours. By transforming the information you want to remember into a relatable story or plot, you tap into the innate human affinity for storytelling, making facts more memorable and accessible. For example, if you are working to memorize a sequence of events in a historical timeline, imagine placing characters in your memory palace who represent specific events sheltering those events under a vivid story arc. This approach transforms abstract dates or facts into compelling narratives that are much easier to recall later.

Visualizations further enhance creativity in your memory palace. When placing new information within your palace, embellish it with vivid imagery that captivates your imagination. For instance, instead of merely thinking of your favorite book, visualize an enormous book on your shelf, surrounded by colorful covers that represent different themes or chapters. Pull in sensory details—different textures, sounds, and even tastes—ensuring that the memory evokes a multi-sensory experience. This rich tapestry of vivid representations strengthens the neural connections associated with that information.

While designing your memory spaces, be mindful of the potential pitfalls associated with excessive personalization. Striking a balance is crucial; individuality should enhance recall rather than clutter your mental pathways with distractions. Avoid cramming too much information into a single location, as popularization can lead to memory overload and confusion. Instead, allocate distinct spaces for various topics or themes within your palace, thereby creating an organized and coherent retrieval environment.

Moreover, regularly reviewing and updating your memory palace is key to maintaining its effectiveness. As knowledge accumulates and develops, returning to your palace to modify it by adding new rooms, characters, or associations will keep the structure relevant and engaging. Embrace the fluidity of these memory systems and allow your creativity to flow as your knowledge base evolves.

To measure the impact of creativity and personalization within your memory palace, document your progress using tools like journaling or digital applications that track your recall performance over time. By evaluating your recall abilities through regular assessments, you can adjust your strategies based on what works best for you and explore new creative avenues to expand your memory skills further.

As you embark on this journey of crafting personalized and creative memory palaces, you're not just building structures to hold information. You're engaging in an enriching process of self-discovery, connecting with your own intellectual style and fostering a more profound sense of ownership and creativity over your learning experience. This personalized approach transforms memory work into a vibrant, dynamic, and deeply meaningful journey toward knowledge retention and cognitive enhancement. Through infusing personal elements into your memory techniques, you will craft spaces that resonate with meaning, allowing you to not just remember but to thrive in the pursuit of learning and understanding.

7.4. Common Pitfalls and Remedies

In navigating the captivating realm of memory palaces, individuals often encounter several common pitfalls that can impede their success in using this powerful mnemonic technique. These pitfalls, while easily overlooked, can significantly detract from the efficacy of memory enhancement efforts. By identifying these stumbling blocks and implementing remedies, one can optimize the overall effectiveness of memory palace construction.

One of the most prevalent pitfalls is the tendency to overload the memory palace with excessive information. When striving to memorize large amounts of content, it can be tempting to cram as much information as possible into each location within the palace. This approach often leads to confusion and a struggle to retrieve specific pieces of information. To remedy this, individuals should aim to compartmentalize their learning. Instead of attempting to store disparate information in a single location, it is helpful to dedicate distinct rooms or areas within the palace to specific topics or themes. For example, if studying for an exam in biology, one might reserve the kitchen for cellular processes while using the living room to remember anatomical structures. This structured organization not only alleviates cognitive overload but also enhances the clarity of recall.

Another common issue arises from a lack of vividness in the imagery employed within the memory palace. Many individuals default to generic or abstract representations of the information they want to remember. Such vague imagery diminishes the effectiveness of the mnemonic device by failing to create strong associative links. The remedy lies in cultivating rich and engaging visualizations that evoke sensory experiences. Incorporate vibrant colors, exaggerated features, and even emotionally charged elements to transform standard facts into memorable representations. For instance, if memorizing the process of photosynthesis, one might envision a sun wearing sunglasses, smiling as it beams down on a field of giant, happy flowers. This kind of vivid imagery will make the information more memorable and accessible.

Emotion also plays a crucial role in memory retention, yet learners sometimes overlook its importance in their memory palaces. Dwelling solely on facts without exploring emotional connections can significantly hinder recall. The remedy involves consciously integrating personal anecdotes, stories, or feelings that tie into the information being memorized. When placing information in memory locations, think about how the material resonates with personal experiences or values. This emotional engagement will help solidify the memories and make the retrieval process more intuitive.

Additionally, individuals might find themselves neglecting to revisit their memory palaces regularly. Memory retention is greatly enhanced by practice and repetition; however, it's common to construct the palace and then forget about it. To combat this pitfall, establish a routine for revisiting and mentally walking through your memory palace. Scheduling regular review sessions will strengthen the memory pathways associated with the information stored within. Remember that memory is not just about encoding; it requires ongoing reinforcement for optimal recall.

Another potential pitfall emerges when individuals become too attached to their original design of the memory palace. As time goes on, the information being recalled may evolve, making some aspects of the palace outdated or irrelevant. It is vital to maintain flexibility and adapt the memory palace as needed. For example, rooms can be reconfigured to accommodate new topics or information. Embrace change and allow the memory palace to evolve alongside your learning journey, thereby ensuring that it remains a relevant and effective tool.

Furthermore, a lack of spatial awareness can hinder the efficacy of the memory palace technique. Since spatial memory is a critical component of this strategy, being unfamiliar with the layout of your chosen space can hamper recall. To remedy this, take some time to mentally walk through each area or room of your memory palace before committing information to it. By immersing yourself in the spatial context, you will enhance the mental mapping that underpins memory retrieval.

Lastly, remember that creating a memory palace requires practice and patience. Many individuals may expect immediate results and become discouraged when they do not see the anticipated improvements in memory recall. This lack of persistence can lead to abandonment of the technique. The remedy is to cultivate a growth mindset and understand that mastery of memory techniques takes time and consistent effort. Set realistic goals and celebrate incremental progress along the way.

In summary, common pitfalls in constructing memory palaces frequently stem from cognitive overload, lack of vivid imagery, neglect of emotional associations, insufficient practice, inflexibility in design, spatial disorientation, and a lack of persistence. By recognizing these challenges and adopting the suggested remedies, individuals can optimize their use of memory palaces as a powerful technique for improving retention and recall. Embrace the nuances of this practice, and with dedication and creativity, you will unlock the door to enhanced memory capabilities that pave the way for lifelong learning and personal growth.

7.5. Measuring Your Progress and Effectiveness

To effectively measure your progress and the effectiveness of your memory enhancement techniques, especially through the use of memory palaces, it is crucial to incorporate a range of evaluation tools and metrics. Here are several strategies and approaches you can employ to assess and optimize how well your memory palace technique operates for you:

1. Self-Assessment of Recall Ability: Start by regularly testing your recall ability. Create a systematic approach for quiz-style assessments where you try to remember items placed in your memory palace. For instance, after populating your palace with information, wait a few days and then mentally revisit each location. Use flashcards or write a list of what you recall from each room. Keep

a journal to document not only the items you remember but also the accuracy and completeness of your recall. This initial assessment helps establish a baseline against which you can measure improvements over time.

2. Use of Retention Metrics: Establish specific metrics to quantify your retention success, such as the percentage of items accurately recalled during assessments. Create a scoring system to gauge your progress based on the number of items remembered correctly versus the total number of items stored in each section of your memory palace. Over time, graph this data to visually track improvements.

3. Consistency Evaluation: Another critical factor in measuring progress is consistency. Assess how frequently you practice recalling the memory palace's contents and how diverse your practice sessions are. Good memory retention is often linked to regular and spaced practice sessions. Note your initial recall abilities immediately after building the palace versus after several refresher sessions. Consider utilizing spaced repetition software or apps to keep your intervals regular and to facilitate evaluations.

4. Emotional Engagement Assessment: Since emotions play a vital role in memory retention, keep track of how emotionally engaged you feel while constructing and recalling your memory palace. This could be established through a simple rating scale that measures your emotional connection to the material. Noting your emotional state may reveal whether certain memory techniques are resonating with you or whether modifications are needed to enhance your engagement.

5. Feedback Mechanisms: Seek feedback from peers or mentors if applicable. Sharing your memory palace experience with others may yield additional insights and constructive criticism about your retention techniques. Engaging in discussions may also

prompt you to think critically about your structure and techniques, offering new angles for improvement.

6. Modification and Adaptation: Measure how well personal modifications or adaptations to your memory palace are yielding results. If you change the visual imagery, the locations used, or the themes established within your palace, track how these adjustments affect your recall ability. Maintaining a log of modifications and results will help identify what works best for you, allowing for ongoing evolution regarding your memorization strategies.

7. Time Trials: Test how quickly you can recall information from your memory palace. Set a timer, and during one practice session, see how long it takes you to walk through your palace mentally and retrieve all stored information. Keep a record of your time over various sessions to determine whether speed improves with practice, indicating a strengthening recall pathway.

8. Contextual Variability: Assess your ability to recall information from your memory palace in different contexts. For example, try recalling the information while in different environments or under varying conditions (like when distracted or stressed). If you can still effectively retrieve the information, this indicates a more robust memory structure.

9. Correlational Studies: If applicable, relate your progress to real-world applications. Note any instances where you successfully utilized information from your memory palace in practical scenarios, such as during presentations or discussions, which reinforces the functional significance of your memory practice.

10. Longitudinal Tracking: Finally, consider a longitudinal approach —record your assessments over weeks, months, or even years to understand how your memory enhancement techniques evolve. Document successes and any dips in retention to identify patterns with your memory skills and application of memory palaces over time.

By creating a comprehensive set of tools and metrics for evaluating your memory palace's effectiveness, you will not only enhance your capacity for recall but also gain critical insights into your cognitive strengths and areas for improvement. Measuring progress in this structured way reinforces the learning and memory enhancement process, leading to greater successes in personal knowledge retention and cognitive application, ultimately transforming your memory palace into a powerful ally in your cognitive journey.

8. Applications of Memory Palaces in Everyday Life

8.1. Academic Excellence and Retention

Academic excellence and retention are cornerstones of successful learning outcomes in educational settings. As students navigate the complexities of academic environments, the strategies they employ to retain knowledge and enhance cognitive performance become increasingly crucial. The integration of memory techniques, particularly the use of memory palaces, represents a powerful means of not just improving academic performance, but also fostering effective long-term retention and understanding.

At the heart of optimizing academic excellence is the acknowledgment that our current educational landscape is laden with information overload. Students are often bombarded with vast amounts of material they are expected to memorize for exams, assignments, and projects. Traditional approaches to learning, which heavily rely on rote memorization, are inadequate for deep, long-term retention of knowledge. Therefore, the need for innovative techniques that engage students in meaningful interactions with content is essential. Memory palaces, derived from ancient mnemonic strategies, are one such technique that enables learners to navigate overwhelming information by associating it within structured, spatial contexts.

In constructing a memory palace, students create a mental representation of a physical space—often one that is familiar to them—and populate it with visual cues tied to the information they wish to retain. This method leverages the brain's spatial memory system, allowing students to 'walk through' their mental space and retrieve lessons and information associated with each locus. Research has indicated that spatial mnemonic devices not only enhance recall but also improve understanding, as students are more likely to relate concepts to broader themes and contexts when visually anchored within a recognizable structure.

For instance, imagine a student preparing for a history exam. They might visualize their childhood home as their memory palace, using each room to represent different historical eras or key figures. In the living room, they might place visualizations of the American Revolution, complete with specific events and dates, while the kitchen could house information about significant treaties. By revisiting this mental structure while studying, the student benefits from both spatial navigation—allowing for quicker recall—and emotional connections fueled by nostalgia and familiarity, enhancing overall academic retention.

Employing a memory palace not only aids in information retention but also fosters active engagement in learning. As students construct their palaces, they engage in deeper cognitive processes such as visualization and narrative construction. These processes cultivate a sense of ownership over the material, making the learning experience more personally meaningful. As the act of creation is coupled with content engagement, information processing becomes more optimized, leading to higher retention rates.

Moreover, academic environments often encourage collaborative learning experiences. Memory palaces can be further enhanced through peer discussions and presentations. By sharing their palaces with classmates, students are prompted to articulate their understanding of the material, which reinforces learning. Revisiting and discussing these memory structures can also allow for the exchange of different perspectives and mnemonic techniques, promoting a culture of collective retention and excellence.

Beyond content retention, the use of memory techniques instills students with valuable metacognitive skills. As they engage in constructing and revising their memory palaces, students become more aware of their learning strategies and the effectiveness of different techniques. This self-awareness enables them to adjust their study habits and adopt better learning frameworks, ensuring lasting academic success.

In addressing the need for academic excellence, it becomes clear that fostering effective retention strategies is not merely about achieving higher grades; it is essential for developing lifelong learners equipped to engage critically with information. Memory palaces provide students a framework not only to excel academically but also to cultivate a deeper understanding of their subject matter.

In conclusion, the integration of memory palaces promotes academic excellence by enabling learners to effectively retain and recall information in a dynamic, engaging, and highly personalized manner. By leveraging spatial awareness, visualization, and collaborative learning, students not only enhance their immediate memory capabilities but also build essential cognitive skills that will serve them well throughout their educational journeys and beyond. As educational strategies continue to evolve, embracing structured mnemonic techniques will play a pivotal role in shaping classrooms where excellence in learning and retention thrives, illuminating the path toward greater intellectual empowerment for every student.

8.2. Professional and Workplace Skills

As we transition into an era characterized by rapid technological advancement and an increasingly competitive professional landscape, the development and enhancement of workplace skills are pivotal for individual success. Memory palaces, a powerful mnemonic tool derived from ancient techniques, can play a crucial role in fostering professional capabilities and integrating cognitive enhancements into everyday work environments. By harnessing the principles of memory palaces, individuals can improve not only their retention of essential information but also their adaptability and effectiveness in a variety of professional settings.

One of the foundational elements of enhancing workplace skills is the ability to retain and recall vast amounts of information relevant to one's job role. Professionals across industries—be it sales, project management, or healthcare—often deal with intricate weighty data, complex ideas, and nuanced details that require high-level recall. Employing memory palaces allows individuals to mentally organize this information in a spatial format, facilitating quicker access when needed. Imagine a salesperson memorizing product specifications; by populating specific locations in a memory palace with distinct features and benefits, the salesperson can effortlessly retrieve this information during client meetings. This not only enhances professional performance but also builds an aura of confidence, showing mastery over their sales materials.

In addition to improving recall, memory palaces can significantly enhance the soft skills that play a vital role in professional interactions. Skills such as effective communication, negotiation, and persuasive storytelling benefit from memory techniques that allow professionals to weave narratives that engage and inform. By crafting memory palaces that include key points, counterarguments, and storytelling nuances, individuals can prepare themselves for high-stakes conversations and presentations. This advanced preparation fosters deeper connections with clients, colleagues, and stakeholders, ultimately enhancing interpersonal effectiveness and fostering collaborative work environments.

Moreover, using memory palaces can support lifelong learning and adaptive skill-building in an ever-changing workplace landscape. Continuous professional development is essential in a world where technology and workplace expectations evolve rapidly. Engaging in the practice of creating and revising memory palaces allows individuals to build a resilient system for acquiring and retaining new skills and knowledge. Whether it involves learning new software, mastering compliance regulations, or adjacent industry knowledge, having a structured and imaginative approach to organizing information empowers professionals to stay agile and effectively tackle fresh challenges.

Another critical aspect of workplace skill enhancement is the capacity to integrate feedback and make iterative improvements. Through the lens of memory palaces, individuals can create a framework for receiving constructive feedback and incorporating it into their practices. For instance, after a presentation or meeting, one can mentally stroll through their memory palace to identify areas for growth by associating specific feedback items with distinct loci. Over time, this reflective practice not only alleviates anxiety surrounding performance but also allows individuals to develop an ongoing habit of self-improvement that promotes accountability and professional growth.

Cultural considerations must also be taken into account when applying memory palaces to workplace settings. Each organization has unique values, language, and communication styles that impact how information is processed and shared. When creating a memory palace, tailoring the content to align with these cultural nuances—such as incorporating industry-specific jargon or culturally relevant analogies—can enhance the resonance and effectiveness of the mnemonic tool. This cultural adaptability builds rapport and fosters an inclusive environment, where all team members feel empowered to participate in knowledge sharing and collaboration.

As we recognize the potential of memory palaces to bolster professional skills, it is essential to emphasize the importance of maintaining a balance between technology and traditional methods. While digital tools facilitate quick access to information, the active engagement of the mind through techniques like memory palaces cultivates a holistic understanding of the material. Encouraging employees to explore both avenues—digital tools for quick reference and memory palaces for proficient retention—can create a more integrated learning approach that fosters deeper mastery of workplace skills.

In summary, incorporating memory palaces into professional development strategies offers a powerful means to enhance workplace skills at multiple levels. From improving information recall and communication abilities to fostering adaptability and self-improvement, this ancient mnemonic technique stands to empower professionals in a modern context. As individuals embrace this blending of creativity and structure, they can cultivate a transformative approach to professional retention, engagement, and excellence, ultimately readying them to thrive in an ever-evolving global landscape. By unlocking the cognitive potential inherent in memory palaces, individuals can elevate their careers and contribute significantly to their organizations —leading to a culture of learning, growth, and sustained success.

8.3. Social Skills and Enhanced Interactions

In our rapidly evolving world, social skills are more essential than ever, playing a pivotal role in personal and professional success. The ability to communicate effectively and connect with others is rooted in a deep understanding of memory—both in retaining essential information and in recalling moments that enhance interpersonal interactions. Memory palaces can serve as innovative tools to enhance social skills, allowing individuals to construct rich cognitive frameworks that facilitate better social engagements, emotional intelligence, and effective relationship-building capabilities.

Establishing social skills involves mastering various components: active listening, empathy, nuanced conversation, and relationship management. Memory techniques, particularly the use of memory palaces, can heighten awareness of these components by promoting a structured approach to retaining important social cues, names, and significant details about the people we interact with. Imagine meeting someone for the first time; by creating a mental palace that associates their name with vivid imagery and elements from conversations you have had, you are not only fostering memory recall but also personalizing interactions in a way that enhances that individual feel valued and recognized.

Active listening, a crucial part of effective communication, can also be supported through structured memory enhancement. By using memory techniques, individuals can better retain details shared during conversations, which allows for meaningful follow-up questions that demonstrate genuine interest and attentiveness. For example, by placing key points of a conversation within the various rooms of your memory palace, your mental 'walk' through these spaces can guide you during a subsequent interaction. Such techniques enable individuals to recall key topics effortlessly, helping them build a narrative thread that is coherent and engaging while imparting the sense of understanding to their conversation partners.

Furthermore, empathy—a core social skill—is enhanced through memory palaces by encouraging individuals to store and retrieve personal experiences that reflect diverse perspectives and emotions. By creating vivid scenes that encapsulate particular emotional experiences or anecdotes, individuals can draw upon this rich tapestry of memories to deepen their empathetic connections with others. For instance, if you vividly remember a time when you felt vulnerable or anxious, recalling that experience can help build bridges with someone going through a similar situation, fostering understanding and establishing rapport. This not only enhances your own emotional intelligence but also enriches your interactions, allowing you to connect with others on a deeper level.

In daily social interactions, we often encounter a whirlwind of necessary information, from personal details about acquaintances to broader social dynamics present in group settings. Memory palaces help individuals navigate this landscape by providing a structured approach to retaining critical details about people's preferences, interests, or past interactions. For example, a manager could utilize a memory palace to remember employees' significant achievements or personal interests, ensuring that they can acknowledge and celebrate milestones during team meetings. This conscious effort to recognize individuals enhances motivation, fosters loyalty, and creates a culture of appreciation within teams.

Moreover, enhancing one's social skills is not solely about retaining information; it also involves practicing and refining specific techniques. By incorporating memory techniques into role-playing scenarios or conversational practice sessions, individuals can rehearse and embed key social strategies into their memory structures. A memory palace can serve as a valuable rehearsal space to practice various conversational techniques, allowing individuals to mentally 'act out' scenarios where active listening or assertiveness plays a key role.

Creativity in personalizing memory palaces can also boost social skills dramatically; visualizing social situations, complete with physical gestures, facial expressions, and tones of voice, provides a multisensory experience that enriches learning. When practicing empathy or conflict resolution, consider designing specific spaces within your memory palace that represent different social scenarios, each populated with diverse personality types. With this approach, individuals can simulate challenging interactions in a safe, imaginative space —fine-tuning their capabilities and preparing emotionally for real-world engagements.

Finally, as cognitive enhancement technologies continue to evolve, exploring digital memory aids integrated with social skill training holds promise for the future. Interactive apps designed around memory palaces can offer guided social skill exercises, encouraging users to enhance memory while actively developing their interpersonal prowess. In creating a shift toward a more engaging and comprehensive approach to memory within social contexts, technology has the potential to make learning adaptable and accessible to diverse populations.

In summary, enhancing social skills through the application of memory principles allows individuals to create personalized memory palaces that facilitate emotional connections, active listening, personalized engagement, and situational rehearsals. By developing these memory structures, people can transition from passive receivers of information to active participants in their social environments, making relationships more meaningful and lasting. In an age where interpersonal connections are paramount, memory palaces stand out as powerful tools for augmenting our social capabilities, preparing us for better communication and enhanced human interactions.

8.4. Boosting Creativity and Problem-Solving

As we delve deeper into the realm of memory enhancement, a particularly intriguing aspect emerges surrounding boosting creativity and problem-solving by employing techniques such as memory palaces. Creativity and problem-solving are vital skills across various domains, from scientific research to artistic expression and everyday decision-making. By understanding and applying memory techniques, individuals can unlock their creative potential and develop more effective solutions to complex issues.

The first step in cultivating creativity through memory enhancement lies in the recognition that memory is not merely a reservoir of facts; it is an active process that interweaves knowledge and experience with imaginative thought. Memory palaces serve as profound tools for enhancing this interplay between memory and creativity. When constructing a memory palace, individuals engage in vivid visualization, creating rich mental landscapes that can act as springboards for innovative ideas. These landscapes are not just storage spaces; they represent dynamic environments where multiple concepts can coexist and interrelate.

To boost creativity within a memory palace, individuals can utilize techniques such as associative thinking. When placing information in different loci or locations, consider how various pieces of knowledge relate or contrast with one another. For instance, if an artist wants to enhance their creative process, they might create a memory palace where each room represents different artistic movements, techniques, or their own works. By juxtaposing these elements within a mental framework, the artist can trigger connections, insights, and novel ideas drawn from the intermingling of disparate concepts.

In addition to linking varied pieces of information, storytelling plays an essential role in fostering creativity within memory palaces. By crafting narratives around the information stored in their palace, individuals engage not just their memory, but their imagination as well. Imagine building a narrative where characters derived from different scientific theories interact with one another. This approach not only consolidates knowledge but ignites creative thought as individuals explore unexpected relationships and outcomes within their narratives. Transforming facts into engaging stories fosters a richer experience and facilitates the flow of ideas—essential components of the creative process.

Moreover, sensory engagement within memory palaces can further amplify creativity. By incorporating vivid sensory details into each remembered location—such as colors, sounds, and emotions—individuals create multi-sensory associations that can stimulate creative thought. The more sensory information tied to an idea, the more robust the memory, allowing for greater avenues of creativity to open. An individual might visualize an inspiring scent associated with the memory of a significant achievement placed in their creative memory palace, bridging a personal experience with an evocative sensory experience that influences current creative endeavors.

Problem-solving skills can be effectively strengthened through the use of memory palaces as well. When faced with a complex issue, constructing a memory palace allows individuals to break down the problem into manageable components, assigning each component to a specific locus. This enables a structured visualization that not only organizes disparate pieces of information but encourages directed brainstorming. By mentally 'walking' through the palace, individuals can explore various facets of the problem and recall relevant knowledge or insights that may influence their final conclusions.

Furthermore, memory palaces facilitate the technique of lateral thinking—a method that encourages unconventional and creative approaches to problem-solving. By cultivating a flexible mindset, individuals nurture a propensity for forging unique connections and considering multiple perspectives. Building a memory palace filled with imaginative associations encourages the exploration of alternative solutions that may not emerge through traditional linear thinking.

It is essential to note that feedback loops are vital in enhancing creativity and problem-solving. Individuals can create memory palaces that reflect not only knowledge but also experiences and outcomes from specific projects. By revisiting their palace and assessing the effectiveness of the different creative approaches they employed, individuals gather insights that feed back into their future endeavors.

This reflective practice enables continuous improvement, reinforcing creative confidence and versatility in problem-solving strategies.

In conclusion, boosting creativity and problem-solving skill sets through the utilization of memory palaces offers profound opportunities for individuals looking to enhance their cognitive capabilities. By intertwining visualization, storytelling, sensory engagement, and structured organization, memory palaces emerge as powerful tools that enable the unlocking of creative potential. As we embrace the techniques of memory enhancement within the realms of creativity and problem-solving, we cultivate a growth-oriented mindset that inspires innovation and facilitates resolution in the multifaceted challenges we encounter in both our personal and professional lives.

8.5. Preparing for Future Challenges

As we find ourselves in a world characterized by rapid change and unpredictability, the importance of preparing for future challenges becomes ever more apparent. The evolution of technology, society, and knowledge demands that we equip ourselves not just with the tools to process current information but with the cognitive agility to adapt to what lies ahead. In this context, memory palaces emerge as a powerful mnemonic technique that facilitates adaptive learning, enabling individuals to retain a vast array of information while honing their cognitive abilities for future applications.

At the core of using memory palaces as a means of preparing for future challenges lies the concept of creating a structured environment that organizes knowledge in a coherent manner. Memory palaces allow individuals to encode information spatially, anchoring details to familiar locations within a mental framework. When facing uncertainty, the ability to access relevant information quickly becomes a critical asset. By systematically associating knowledge with designated loci, learners can build cognitive pathways that promote easy retrieval of insights when navigating complex scenarios.

Moreover, the process of constructing a memory palace fosters creative thinking and problem-solving skills. As individuals design their palaces, they engage in visual and imaginative exercises that stimulate divergent thinking—the ability to explore multiple solutions and perspectives. This creative engagement empowers individuals to think outside the box, embracing varied approaches to challenges. For example, if a business professional is tasked with developing a strategic plan in uncertain market conditions, they could use a memory palace to explore potential tactics, associating each room with distinct strategies or scenarios. This multi-faceted exploration enhances the mental toolbox from which creative and effective solutions can be drawn.

Additionally, memory palaces can serve as repositories of knowledge that prepare individuals for the necessity of lifelong learning. In an era where new information is continuously emerging, being able to store and recall relevant knowledge quickly is paramount. By utilizing memory palaces, learners can cultivate a flexible and agile approach to acquiring new information, adapting their palaces to accommodate evolving knowledge bases. This adaptability ensures that individuals remain equipped to tackle future challenges with confidence, as the learning process becomes integrated into their cognitive architecture.

The efficacy of memory palaces in preparing for future challenges is further enhanced by their versatility across various domains. Whether in academic settings, professional environments, or personal development, memory techniques can be tailored to suit specific learning objectives. For students, this might mean constructing a palace to navigate the intricate details of a complex subject. For professionals, it could mean anchoring insights from conferences or workshops for practical application. Across all contexts, the ability to organize and retrieve information effectively will undoubtedly bolster individual performance and readiness to confront challenges.

One crucial aspect of leveraging memory palaces for future challenges involves fostering an awareness of the emotional landscape associated with learning. The brain's processing of information is heavily influenced by emotional states, and memory palaces can harness this connection by incorporating emotionally significant experiences and narratives. Building narratives around the information stored in a memory palace creates contexts that resonate, strengthening both memory retention and emotional intelligence. In preparing for potential challenges, understanding the emotional dimensions tied to information can provide invaluable insights for navigating interpersonal relations and decision-making.

Moreover, embracing retrospection as a fundamental element of memory palace practice can amplify its effectiveness. Regularly revisiting a memory palace can be framed as an opportunity for reflection on past experiences. This reflective process encourages individuals to savor their learning journeys, identify key insights, and draw lessons from previous challenges encountered. By decoding experiences and embedding newfound knowledge into their palaces, learners enhance their capacity to adapt and approach future uncertainties with proactive strategies.

Lastly, as we prepare for the future, it becomes increasingly important to integrate memory techniques with emerging technologies. The convergence of memory palaces with digital tools such as virtual reality, augmented reality, and AI offers immense potential for enhancing adaptive learning experiences. Such tools can create immersive memory environments, amplifying the mental engagement process. Collaboration among technologists and cognitive practitioners can yield innovations that augment memory capabilities, allowing future generations to thrive in an era of constant change.

In conclusion, preparing for future challenges through the mastery of memory palaces provides individuals with a dynamic framework for cognitive enhancement. By cultivating structured memory architectures, fostering creativity, embracing emotional engagement, promoting lifelong learning, and integrating technology into these practices, we equip ourselves to navigate unpredictability with resilience and adaptability. Memory palaces stand as powerful instruments—not only facilitating the retention of knowledge, but also empowering individuals to forge meaningful connections, explore innovative ideas, and develop the skills necessary to face the complexities of the future.

As we embark on this journey of cognitive mastery, we encourage readers to embrace the art of memory palaces as a vital strategy ensuring that the power of memory becomes a cornerstone for facing challenges yet to come.

9. Augmenting Intelligence: Beyond Memory

9.1. Understanding Intelligence

Understanding intelligence is a multifaceted endeavor that intertwines historical perspectives, contemporary theories, and emerging paradigms. Intelligence, traditionally defined as the cognitive ability to learn, reason, solve problems, and adapt to new situations, is not merely a measure of one's knowledge or skills, but a complex interplay of various cognitive processes, emotional capacities, and social interactions. This exploration aims to unpack the various dimensions of intelligence—ranging from logical reasoning and problem-solving to emotional and social intelligence—offering a holistic understanding of an individual's intellectual capacity.

Historically, intelligence has been approached through a variety of lenses. Theories of intelligence, such as Howard Gardner's Multiple Intelligences, challenge the conventional notion of a singular, fixed intelligence quotient (IQ). Gardner posits that individuals possess multiple intelligences, including linguistic, logical-mathematical, spatial, musical, interpersonal, intrapersonal, bodily-kinesthetic, and naturalistic intelligences. Recognizing these distinct forms allows for a broader appreciation of human capabilities and the recognition that traditional IQ tests may overlook significant areas of a person's cognitive strengths.

Emotional intelligence (EI), another key dimension, emphasizes the importance of recognizing, understanding, and managing one's emotions as well as the emotions of others. Daniel Goleman, a leading authority in this field, argues that EI is critical for success in both personal and professional realms. This perspective shifts the focus from cognitive intelligence alone to the integration of emotional skills, making the case that a person's ability to navigate social environments, empathize with others, and regulate their emotional responses is paramount for holistic intelligence. By understanding and developing emotional intelligence, individuals are better equipped to forge meaningful relationships and foster collaborative environments.

Cognitive science, a rich interdisciplinary field merging psychology, neuroscience, linguistics, and philosophy, further elucidates the mechanics of intelligence. Current research in cognitive science explores how intelligence interacts with memory, learning processes, and brain function. For instance, neuroplasticity—the brain's ability to adapt and rewire itself based on experience—has profound implications for how we understand intelligence. The more we learn and engage in cognitive activities, the more our brains can develop new connections. This principle highlights the potential for intelligence to be cultivated and enhanced over time, rather than being a static trait determined at birth.

The advent of digital technology has introduced new dimensions to the discussion of intelligence. With knowledge readily accessible through the internet, individuals are learning to navigate how information is acquired, processed, and used intelligently. The modern landscape necessitates a form of digital intelligence, where individuals must discern reliable information sources, advocate for ethical digital citizenship, and adeptly use technology to foster learning and collaboration. This context has led to a reassessment of what it means to be intelligent in a world of information overload.

Furthermore, as artificial intelligence (AI) continues to develop, the relationship between human intelligence and machine intelligence has become a subject of extensive debate. The implications of AI on our understanding of intelligence challenge the traditional boundaries of what it means to be intelligent. By defining intelligence through the lens of adaptability, reasoning, and problem-solving, we see emerging questions about the uniqueness of human cognition. As AI systems begin to demonstrate capabilities traditionally associated with human thought, such as learning and decision-making, we must grapple with the ethical implications of these technologies and how they may complement or even augment human intelligence.

In addition to these dimensions, cultural context plays a vital role in shaping our understanding of intelligence. Different cultures may prioritize various attributes deemed intelligent, from communal problem-solving abilities to individual initiative. This cultural diversity enriches the definition of intelligence by illustrating that it is not universally defined but rather shaped by societal values, norms, and expectations.

As we contemplate the future of intelligence—both human and artificial—there lies an exciting interplay between cognitive neuroscience and technology. The integration of educational tools and cognitive enhancements can lead to profound advancements in training cognitive skills. For instance, memory techniques such as memory palaces can be utilized as cognitive enhancement tools to support learners in their pursuit of increased intelligence. By fostering cognitive engagement through structured emotional and social learning frameworks, contemporary society can cultivate intelligent individuals who are not only adept at reasoning but are also capable of empathy, adaptability, and collaborative problem-solving.

In summary, understanding intelligence goes beyond mere academic knowledge to encompass various cognitive, emotional, social, and cultural dimensions. Emphasizing the diversity of intelligences, as well as the relationship between human and machine intelligence, illustrates the efficacy of a comprehensive approach. As this exploration unfolds, we embrace the intricate tapestry of human cognition, recognizing that intelligence is a dynamic, evolving construct—one that we are continuously redefining in our increasingly complex world. By engaging with this comprehensive understanding, we equip ourselves to appreciate the potential for cognitive growth and the advancements of intelligence in shaping our future.

9.2. Cognitive Enhancements and Their Effects

Cognitive enhancements, which encompass various techniques and tools designed to improve memory and overall cognitive function, have garnered significant interest in contemporary society. These enhancements arise from an evolving understanding of the brain and have profound implications for various aspects of life, including education, work, and personal development. The effects of cognitive enhancements, especially through the use of techniques like memory palaces, digital tools, and advancements in neuroscience, reflect a multifaceted approach to optimizing brain function.

To begin with, cognitive enhancements rooted in memory techniques like the Method of Loci have demonstrated significant efficacy in improving retention and recall. Memory palaces allow individuals to create vivid mental representations by associating information with specific spatial locations. This technique leverages our innate familiarity with navigation and enhances retrieval of stored knowledge, effectively transforming abstract data into relatable experiences. This spatial encoding caters to our brain's natural capabilities, leading to lasting improvements in memory performance.

Moreover, the advent of digital technologies presents new opportunities for memory enhancement. Various applications leverage the principles of spaced repetition, gamification, and interactive learning, enabling users to optimize their cognitive training. These tools extend beyond traditional memory methods, providing adaptive learning environments that cater to individual preferences and needs. In doing so, they empower users to take an active role in their cognitive development, leading to improved retention and recall of information in diverse contexts.

Research indicates that cognitive enhancements impact not only memory but also overall cognitive function, including problem-solving abilities, attentional control, and processing speed. Techniques that promote cognitive flexibility—such as visual imagery, brainstorming within structured environments, and active engagement with material—contribute to better adaptability and creativity. This adaptability is vital in a rapidly changing world where individuals are often required to navigate complex challenges.

Furthermore, research in neuroscience underlines the significant role of neuroplasticity in cognitive enhancement. The brain's ability to form new connections and reorganize itself based on experience provides a biological foundation for the effectiveness of enhancement techniques. Regular practice of cognitive enhancements fosters these neural changes, allowing individuals to not just retain information but also improve the underlying cognitive processes associated with memory and learning.

The effects of cognitive enhancements extend into everyday life, impacting social interactions and professional performance. Enhanced memory capabilities empower individuals to connect meaningfully with others, fostering better communication practices and the ability to recall important details about co-workers or clients. This relational aspect of enhanced memory promotes stronger working relationships and contributes to a collaborative work environment. As such, cognitive enhancements are not merely about individual improvement but reflect the potential for positive ripple effects on interpersonal dynamics.

However, there are potential pitfalls to cognitive enhancements that must be considered. The risk of over-reliance on digital tools, as well as the ethical implications of memory augmentation techniques, necessitates careful navigation. Individuals must strive to engage with enhancements thoughtfully and maintain a balance between technology-assisted methods and intrinsic cognitive skills.

In summary, cognitive enhancements and their effects are multidimensional, encompassing improvements in memory retention, adaptability, creativity, and interpersonal skills. By leveraging techniques like memory palaces alongside emerging technologies, individuals can unlock their cognitive potential and better prepare themselves to face the challenges of contemporary society. Continual research and engagement with these enhancement methods pave the way for a future where memory and cognitive processes flourish, ultimately enriching personal and collective experiences.

9.3. Intelligence in the Digital Era

In the ever-evolving landscape of the digital age, the interplay between intelligence and technology has achieved new heights, leading to profound changes in our understanding of human cognition. As we sweep through the array of advancements that define the current era, it becomes evident that intelligence is no longer deemed a static trait; rather, it is a malleable construct influenced extensively by digital innovations, cognitive sciences, and our everyday interactions with technology.

The integration of technology into daily life has deeply shaped our perception of intelligence. Where once intelligence was often equated with raw cognitive ability or standardized IQ scores, technology has ushered in a more nuanced understanding. Intelligence is now seen as multidimensional, encompassing not just logical reasoning or problem-solving skills, but also emotional and social intelligence. As artificial intelligence (AI) systems demonstrate remarkable capabilities —ranging from natural language processing to complex data analysis —the traditional definitions of intelligence are being challenged. This raises questions about what it means to be intelligent in an era where machines can learn and adapt in ways that parallel human thought.

As we venture deeper into the digital era, the role of cognitive enhancement techniques becomes increasingly significant. Memory palaces, a method often rooted in ancient mnemonic strategies, exemplify how individuals can leverage their cognitive abilities alongside advancements in technology. By creating vivid mental spaces to organize and retrieve information, learners can tap into their memory's full potential. These memory techniques not only serve as powerful learning aids but also form the foundation upon which individuals can build their intelligence through exploration and comprehension of increasingly complex ideas.

The emergence of AI as a partner to human cognition further complicates our understanding of intelligence in this digital landscape. The notion of merging human and machine intelligence prompts exciting possibilities in cognitive augmentation. AI systems that can analyze user behavior, preferences, and challenges have the potential to create highly personalized learning environments. By generating tailored content and adapting to individual styles of learning, AI can empower people to enhance their cognitive skills dynamically. This partnership could redefine educational practices, knowledge retention, and even collaborative problem-solving.

Nevertheless, alongside these optimistic prospects lie significant considerations. Ethical implications around cognitive enhancement demand thoughtful exploration. As individuals become more reliant on technology to enhance their cognitive processes, the boundaries between human cognition and artificial intelligence blur, prompting critical debates on privacy, fairness, and autonomy. How do we ensure that technology serves as a testament to human ingenuity, rather than diluting our inherently unique cognitive qualities?

As we look toward the future, the potential for aligned intelligence —where human cognition and technological capabilities are harmonized—sparks curiosity and anticipation. We stand on the brink of a new chapter in cognitive evolution, where enhancements may not only improve memory retention but reshape our understanding of learning and intelligence itself. Advances in neuroscience may uncover new mechanisms for integrating human thought with AI algorithms, creating synergistic systems that revolutionize the ways we think, learn, and connect.

In summary, the digital era has redefined intelligence as a complex, dynamic interplay of cognitive processes, social awareness, and technological integration. Memory, as a core component of intelligence, has adapted to contemporary challenges and opportunities. By embracing innovative techniques alongside functional partnerships with technology, we can enrich our understanding of what it means to be intelligent. As we progress into the future, the exploration into intelligence—rooted in memory and interwoven with technology—will undoubtedly hold pivotal implications for personal growth, societal development, and the collective journey of human cognition.

9.4. Merging Human and Machine Cognition

In an age where the boundaries between human intelligence and machine learning are increasingly blurring, the integration of human and machine cognition offers revolutionary possibilities for enhancing memory, problem-solving, and overall cognitive functionality. As we move forward, understanding this convergence of human brain dynamics with technological advancements becomes essential for unlocking new potentials in cognitive enhancement, learning, and memory retention.

At the heart of merging human cognition with machine intelligence is the opportunity to augment the innate capabilities of the human brain. Artificial intelligence technologies can process vast amounts of data at high speeds, analyze patterns, and provide insights that complement human reasoning, thereby supporting decision-making processes. This collaborative framework can create rich interactive environments where human creativity meets machine efficiency, transforming the way we approach tasks like learning and memory recall.

For instance, AI-powered tools can be tailored to individual learning preferences, providing personalized feedback and adaptive memory training exercises. As users engage in memory techniques such as memory palaces or spaced repetition through augmented reality, AI can analyze responses and learning curves to recommend specific memory strategies that optimize retention. This adaptive learning approach allows individuals to leverage the strengths of both their cognitive processes and the analytical capabilities of AI, leading to enhanced memory performance and cognitive growth.

Moreover, the integration of machine cognition can lead to innovative memory augmentation processes, such as brain-computer interfaces (BCIs). These interfaces might allow for direct communication between brain signals and computational devices, enabling real-time memory enhancement and cognitive feedback. By detecting when a user struggles to recall information, BCIs can present alternative cues or activate specific neural pathways, facilitating smoother retrieval.

The potential applications for such technologies range from academic settings—where students could more effortlessly access learned material—to professional environments where individuals can efficiently manage complex project details.

Furthermore, utilizing machine intelligence can help combat cognitive overload, a common issue in today's fast-paced information landscape. By providing structured platforms that filter relevant information and present it in digestible formats, machine cognition can relieve cognitive burdens. For instance, leveraging AI-supported digital tools allows users to develop memory palaces more efficiently, focusing on essential data without sifting through overwhelming amounts of information.

However, the merger of human cognition and machine intelligence does not come without its challenges. Ethical implications surrounding data privacy, autonomy, and reliance on technology must be carefully considered. As users entrust sensitive personal information to technological platforms, ensuring the protection of this data becomes paramount. Moreover, an overreliance on machine intelligence could lead to a decline in intrinsic cognitive abilities; therefore, maintaining a balance between using technology as an enhancement tool while fostering individuals' natural cognitive skills remains critical.

Educational systems can also benefit from merging cognitive techniques with artificial intelligence. Curricula that incorporate personalized learning and cognitive enhancements via machine intelligence can empower students to take charge of their educational journeys. This involves equipping them with tools that promote self-directed learning, engage emotionally with content, and foster creative thinking. By understanding the interplay between human and machine cognition, educators can create enriching environments where students not only strive for academic excellence but cultivate essential life skills.

As we continue to explore the implications of merging human and machine cognition, it becomes increasingly apparent that this convergence has the potential to redefine our approach to memory and intelligence enhancement. By building frameworks that incorporate the nuances of human cognitive processes alongside the efficiency of machine learning, we can pave the way for innovative applications that ultimately foster greater understanding, adaptability, and creativity.

The future beckons exciting collaborative possibilities—where leveraging human distinctiveness combined with AI's processing power will unlock cognitive potentials previously unimagined, leading to a richer experience in learning and expanding the horizons of human intelligence. By navigating this landscape thoughtfully, we can create systems that not only augment but celebrate the capabilities inherent in human cognition, ensuring a harmonious future where innovation and intelligence coalesce to propel us into new realms of discovery.

9.5. Future Intentions for Intelligence Unification

As we envision the future of cognitive enhancement and intelligence unification, our intentions are guided by the convergence of innovative technologies, an enriched understanding of neuroscience, and the potential to redefine human cognition. Central to this future is the aspiration to cultivate enhanced intelligence that intertwines memory, creativity, emotional intelligence, and interpersonal skills. The exploration of intelligence unification opens the door to exciting possibilities, presenting a landscape where human cognitive capabilities become empowered through technology without compromising our unique essence.

At the forefront of these future intentions is the goal to create personalized cognitive enhancement frameworks that adapt to individual needs, strengths, and learning styles. As artificial intelligence and machine learning systems evolve, they can analyze personal cognitive profiles and learning behaviors, offering tailored strategies that optimize memory retention and cognitive flexibility. This adaptive approach encourages individuals to take ownership of their learning journey, inspiring innovative practices that align with their specific goals. By harnessing insights from cognitive science and technology, we strive to build systems that cater to diversity, empowering learners to unlock their full cognitive potential.

Moreover, the future of intelligence unification encompasses the integration of various forms of intelligence—cognitive, emotional, and social—into a cohesive framework for development. In a world that increasingly values collaboration, empathy, and creativity, fostering emotional intelligence alongside traditional measures of cognitive ability becomes paramount. As memory techniques such as memory palaces are harnessed not just for academic success but for holistic personal growth, individuals will flourish in environments that prioritize emotional regulation and relational skills, enabling them to navigate the complexities of both personal and professional landscapes.

Another intention for the future is to establish collaborative ventures among researchers, educators, technologists, and policymakers to craft a comprehensive framework for intelligence enhancement. As global challenges necessitate interdisciplinary approaches, fostering partnerships across various sectors will enable us to pool resources, ideas, and expertise. Through collaborative innovations, we can translate psychological research into practical applications, ensuring that cognitive enhancement techniques are accessible and impactful for all. This concerted effort will lay the groundwork for forward-thinking policies that support equity and inclusion in cognitive advancements.

Furthermore, as we navigate the intersection of human and machine cognition, ethical frameworks will be vital to ensuring responsible development. The future must prioritize individual autonomy, privacy, and informed consent as we embrace the blending of technology with cognitive processes. By cultivating transparent practices and fostering dialogue about the implications of cognitive enhancements, we can build trust and promote safe, ethical advancements that genuinely benefit society.

Memory enhancement techniques will continue to evolve, adapting to fit our increasingly digital landscape. As societal norms shift and lifestyles change, the tools we use to bolster memory—whether through mobile applications, virtual reality experiences, or AI-assisted platforms—will need to remain flexible. We envision a future where memory techniques are seamlessly integrated into daily routines, making cognitive enhancement an intrinsic part of the learning experience, regardless of age, background, or learning style.

As we consider advancements in medical and psychological research, the impact of health perspectives on memory enhancement cannot be overlooked. Future intentions will involve prioritizing the interconnection between physical health and cognitive capabilities, promoting a holistic view of wellbeing. Emphasizing the importance of lifestyle choices, mental health initiatives, and brain health will forge a stronger foundation for cognitive enhancement, ensuring that individuals can thrive in their pursuit of knowledge and self-improvement.

Ultimately, as we look ahead, our intention for intelligence unification is rooted in the belief that enhancing human cognition is not only about retaining information but also about enriching the very fabric of human experience. By melding advances in technology, neuroscience, and emotional intelligence, we can cultivate an intelligence that is adaptable, empathetic, and creatively rich—a synthesis of human potential and technological innovation.

The future of cognitive enhancement beckons a profound journey of exploration, where memory serves as a bridge to understanding the multifaceted dimensions of intelligence. As we embark on this path, we embrace the possibilities that lie ahead, nurturing a world where the collective intelligence of humanity is celebrated and empowered, paving the way for a transformative evolution in how we learn, think, and connect.

10. Memory Reboot: From Science Fiction to Science Fact

10.1. Inspirations from Popular Culture

In popular culture, various mediums such as films, literature, and television have profoundly shaped public perceptions and conceptions of memory and cognitive enhancement. These narratives not only entertain but also provoke thought and discussion about the possibilities and ethical implications of manipulating memory. Popular culture has served as both an imaginative playground and a mirror reflecting societal fears, hopes, and values regarding memory augmentation and intelligence enhancement.

Popular films like "Eternal Sunshine of the Spotless Mind" explore the emotional repercussions of erasing specific memories, presenting a narrative that raises profound questions about the nature of identity and the ethical boundaries of cognitive manipulation. By showcasing the struggle of characters who grapple with their memories, the film encourages viewers to consider the integral role that memories—both positive and negative—play in shaping our identities. The portrayal of memory erasure and its consequences invites contemplation about whether certain experiences, even those that may seem painful, are essential for personal growth and emotional authenticity. This film, among others, highlights the complex relationship between memory and self-identity, prompting public discussions that transcend the screen into everyday considerations.

Similarly, in literature, works such as "The Giver" by Lois Lowry present dystopian societies where memory and emotional experiences are suppressed for the sake of stability and uniformity. The protagonist's awakening to the complexities of memory illustrates the potential dangers of erasing pain and emotion in a bid for control and societal order. By weaving narratives that emphasize the richness and unpredictability of human experience, such stories challenge audiences to value the totality of memories as vital components of life, irrespective of their perceived quality.

Television series like "Black Mirror" probe the darker sides of memory augmentation technologies, exploring scenarios where individuals can record and replay memories at will. These thought-provoking stories often highlight the ethical dilemmas surrounding consent, privacy, and the commodification of memory. They compel viewers to interrogate the balance between innovation and ethical responsibility in cognitive enhancement, ultimately shaping public dialogue about the implications of merging technology with human cognition.

The influence of gaming culture, where players often engage with narratives involving memory and identity, cannot be overlooked. Games like "Remember Me" and "Life is Strange" incorporate memory manipulation as a core mechanic, allowing players to explore how memories influence choices, relationships, and character growth. These interactive experiences immerse players in the emotional weight of remembering, urging them to consider how memories inform their actions and connections with others.

In these ways, popular culture serves as a vehicle that communicates societal attitudes toward memory and cognitive enhancement, instilling curiosity and fostering critical thought about the merits and hazards of advancing technologies. By painting vivid narratives that explore the psychological, emotional, and ethical facets of memory manipulation, these cultural artifacts not only influence public perception but also push for a conscientious examination of the path forward.

The varying representations of memory in popular culture call for a multidimensional understanding of how society embraces or resists advancements in cognitive enhancement. They highlight the need for dialogues that navigate the implications of these technologies, ensuring that memories—our links to identity, experience, and humanity —remain held in reverence as we step into an era defined by the profound interplay of memory and innovation. Through this intricate tapestry woven by popular culture, we are encouraged to contemplate not only what it means to remember but also how those memories shape our collective future in the realm of cognitive enhancement. As we embark on this journey of exploration, the insights gleaned from cultural narratives will guide our quest for knowledge in the realms of memory and intelligence augmentation.

10.2. From Imagination to Innovation

As our world races toward a future defined by innovation and technological advancement, the possibilities of enhancing human cognition and memory through structured techniques become not only fascinating but essential. Welcome to "Memory Palaces of the Future," a journey that explores the ground-breaking methods and intriguing theories shaping our understanding of memory and intelligence augmentation. In this book, we delve into a blend of ancient mnemonic techniques and cutting-edge cognitive sciences, creating a bridge where modern science meets age-old wisdom.

Imagine walking through a palace of your own design, where each room holds secrets to the information you wish to retain, every corridor echoing with the knowledge of your choosing. More than a metaphor, these memory palaces represent a practical framework for storing and recalling information with unprecedented clarity and speed. This book aims to equip you with the tools not just to imagine but to manifest such palaces as potent vectors for personal and intellectual growth.

Join me as we navigate the complex yet incredibly rewarding terrain of cognitive enhancement. This introductory chapter sets the stage for the expansive journey ahead, promising revelations that are often as inspiring as they are practical. So, are you ready to unlock the true potential of your mind? The future of your memory awaits.

In understanding the journey from imagination to innovation, we begin by recognizing that the seeds of great ideas are often sown in creative thought processes—moments when we dare to envision alternatives, challenge conventions, and explore new possibilities. This evolution of thought can take on many forms, but at its essence, it rests on the imagination's ability to draw connections between disparate concepts, thus setting the stage for innovation.

Memory palaces exemplify this journey, merging imaginative visualization with cognitive architecture—transforming our engagement with memories into dynamic, accessible resources.

The first step in this transformation involves cultivating an imaginative mindset, where exploration of ideas knows no bounds. As we delve into the realm of memory techniques, nurturing creativity becomes crucial. It is within the imaginative landscape that our memory palaces take form—places where knowledge is not only retained but also interwoven with narratives and emotions that amplify its significance. By drawing upon our creative faculties, we learn to fabricate intricate mental structures that serve as scaffolds for knowledge, bridging the gap between mere memorization and authentic understanding.

Once we have established imaginative platforms, the next phase involves harnessing those creative impulses to foster innovation. As we visualize our memory palaces, we engage in active design—consciously shaping spaces and details that resonate personally. Each room within our palace becomes a reflection of our unique learning journeys, incorporating individual experiences, interests, and values. This act of personalization enhances our cognitive engagement, prompting us to invest greater emotional energy into learning, which ultimately shapes our capacity for recall.

Furthermore, the interplay between imagination and innovation becomes evident through exploration of diverse perspectives. Embracing interdisciplinary approaches fosters connections between fields, allowing for creative cross-pollination of ideas that transcend traditional boundaries. Within our memory palaces, we can curate a collection of concepts and inspirations from various domains—art, science, philosophy—that inform our understanding of the world and enhance our cognitive flexibility. This exposure not only enriches our mental inventory but also nurtures an innovative spirit that propels us toward new avenues of inquiry.

As we navigate the practical applications of imagination within our memory palaces, it becomes imperative to emphasize the trial-and-error process inherent in innovation. Successful innovation rarely occurs in a vacuum; it requires experimentation, adjustments, and the courage to learn from setbacks. In constructing memory palaces, we can adopt a growth mindset, viewing our initial attempts as blueprints for future enhancements. By regularly revisiting and refining our mental structures, we cultivate a resilience that prepares us to adapt our cognitive strategies in the face of new challenges.

Moreover, leveraging technological advancements alongside imaginative processes opens new realms of possibility for innovation. Tools such as augmented reality (AR) and virtual reality (VR) can elevate our engagement, transforming traditional memory palace methods into immersive experiences. Imagine stepping into a 3D-rendered memory palace, where tactile interactions and dynamic visuals blur the line between imagination and reality. These technologies provide an interactive path toward cognitive enhancement, facilitating deeper engagement and retention while allowing us to reimagine the boundaries of memory.

In summary, the journey from imagination to innovation embodies the essence of memory augmentation and cognitive enhancement through memory palaces. By fostering imaginative thinking and creative exploration, we establish the foundations for innovative practices that transform learning experiences. As we continue to embrace the convergence of creativity and memory enhancement, we unlock untapped potential within our cognitive landscapes, paving the way for future discoveries—both personally and collectively. Together, let us embark on this journey and realize the boundless possibilities that lie at the intersection of imagination and innovation.

10.3. Hero's Journey: Our Inner Scientist

In the pursuit of cognitive enhancement, the concept of the "Hero's Journey" invites us into a unique exploration of our inner scientist —a metaphorical representation of our capacity for experimentation, growth, and discovery in the realm of memory and cognition. Just as the heroes in ancient myths embark on transformative journeys, overcoming challenges and achieving personal insight, we too can embark on a journey of self-exploration through the mastery of cognitive enhancement techniques.

The hero often begins their journey in the ordinary world, where comfort and familiarity exist but are tinged with a sense of yearning for something greater. Likewise, individuals often find themselves in a world filled with distractions and information overload, where the desire for enhanced memory and cognitive performance emerges as a response to everyday challenges. This yearning becomes the catalyst that ignites the quest for knowledge and understanding—much like the hero's call to adventure.

As we embark on this inner journey, we encounter various mentors along the way. These mentors represent the guiding principles of cognitive science, memory techniques, and ancient wisdom that provide essential tools for enhancing our cognitive abilities. Principles like the Method of Loci, spaced repetition, and the integration of emotional intelligence serve as our mentors, guiding us through the complexities of information retention and recall. Through practice and persistence, we learn to navigate the landscape of cognitive enhancement effectively.

However, any journey worth taking is fraught with trials and tribulations. As we strive to adopt memory-enhancing techniques, we may experience challenges such as self-doubt, struggle with information overload, or falter in our practice. These obstacles compel us to confront our beliefs about memory and intelligence, transforming our mindset as we inevitably realize that growth often resides outside of our comfort zones. Overcoming these challenges mirrors the inner turmoil faced by heroes—provoking growth, resilience, and self-discovery.

As we persist in our endeavors, we may encounter the transformative moment often characterized as the hero's "reward" or "awakening." Within the context of memory enhancement, this pivotal turning point manifests as a profound realization of our capabilities to retain and retrieve information, leading us to make unexpected connections between ideas. Much like heroes who emerge from their adventures with newfound wisdom, we develop a sense of empowerment and adaptability that enhances not only our cognitive abilities but also our understanding of ourselves.

The culmination of our journey leads us to a deeper comprehension of the interconnectedness of memory, learning, and cognition. We emerge not only as skilled in the art of memory enhancement through techniques like memory palaces but as enlightened individuals ready to apply our newfound cognitive abilities in diverse contexts—academia, professional environments, and personal relationships. The hero's journey ultimately drives us to share our experiences, insights, and learned strategies with others, fostering a community of knowledge-sharing that encourages growth and collaboration.

While this journey may not follow a rigid path, it is essential to recognize that each individual's experience is uniquely personal. The exploration of our inner scientist highlights the importance of creativity, adaptability, and emotional engagement as we navigate the complexities of the cognitive landscape. Just as heroes return to their ordinary world transformed by their journey, we too can embrace a renewed perspective on memory and intelligence, ready to confront the challenges of a fast-paced world equipped with effective tools for cognitive enhancement.

In conclusion, the Hero's Journey symbolizes our inner scientist's quest—a transformative exploration of the depths of our cognitive capabilities and a commitment to embracing memory-enhancing strategies. By embarking on this journey, we not only cultivate our memory skills but also uncover the powerful, adaptive nature of human cognition. Through determination, resilience, and the pursuit of knowledge, we become not just wiser memory keepers but active participants in the ongoing evolution of human intelligence.

10.4. Pioneers and Innovators in Memory Research

The study of memory has seen a rich history of pioneering researchers and innovators who have shaped our understanding of cognitive function and memory techniques. From the realms of ancient mnemonic systems to contemporary neuroscience, these trailblazers have explored and expanded our comprehension of how memory works, how it can be enhanced, and how it plays a critical role in human cognition.

One of the earliest figures in the field of mémoire is ancient Greek philosopher Simonides of Ceos, who is often credited with originating the memory palace technique, known formally as the Method of Loci. The story goes that after a disastrous collapse of a banquet hall where he was attending a gathering, Simonides was able to identify victims by visualizing their seating positions in the hall, revealing the powerful connection between memory and spatial awareness. This foundational insight led to the understanding that mental imagery and spatial organization are vital for memory retention, principles that continue to influence cognitive enhancement practices today.

In the late 19th and early 20th centuries, memory became a central focus of experimental psychology with pioneers like Hermann Ebbinghaus, who conducted extensive research on the processes of memorization and forgetting. His groundbreaking work led to the formulation of the "forgetting curve" and demonstrated that spaced repetition significantly enhances retention. Ebbinghaus's findings laid the groundwork for many modern techniques in memory enhancement, influencing not only educational practices but also our understanding of human learning processes.

Alongside Ebbinghaus, William James, often regarded as the father of psychology, contributed to the foundational theories of memory with his emphasis on associationism—the notion that memories are interconnected, relying on the principles of association. His extensive writings suggested that memory retrieval is closely tied to how memories are encoded and associated with additional context or experiences. This insight paved the way for later explorations into complex memory networks.

The mid-20th century ushered in another significant figure—George A. Miller—with his influential paper, "The Magical Number Seven, Plus or Minus Two," which proposed that the capacity of working memory tends to be limited to about seven items. Miller's findings prompted further research into cognitive load theory, influencing both theoretical and practical approaches to learning, retention, and memory enhancement.

In the realm of cognitive neuroscience, contemporary innovators such as Daniel Kahneman, known for his groundbreaking work in behavioral economics, elucidated the impacts of cognitive biases on decision-making processes, reflecting on how our understanding of memory is influenced by various factors. Kahneman's insights emphasize that memory is not merely about recall; it also encompasses the cognitive processes that inform our judgments. His research underscores the necessity of addressing how memory interacts with emotional and contextual cues to form our understanding of experiences.

Moreover, the advent of advanced imaging technology has transformed memory research in exciting ways. Researchers like Brenda Milner have conducted influential studies on the neurological underpinnings of memory, particularly through her work with patients such as Henry Molaison (H.M.). Milner's research demonstrated the distinction between different types of memory, particularly the difference between declarative and non-declarative (procedural) memory, and laid the groundwork for understanding the role of the hippocampus in forming new memories.

More recently, pioneers like Elizabeth Loftus have showcased the intricacies of memory accuracy and the malleability of human recollection. Through her groundbreaking work on false memories, Loftus unveiled that memory is not a static entity but rather susceptible to modification, highlighting the implications this has for eyewitness testimony and broader understanding of the nature of human cognition.

In this modern era, the intersection of cognitive science and technology has birthed innovative applications that reflect the work of these pioneers. Memory training apps, digital platforms for interactive learning, and AI-driven personalized learning experiences are emerging based on foundational principles laid down by earlier memory research. The ongoing pursuit of cognitive enhancement through memory technologies continues to advance knowledge-sharing practices, empowering individuals to harness the knowledge of past innovators while shaping pathways for future developments.

As we reflect on the trajectory of memory research, it becomes evident that these pioneers and innovators, through their diverse contributions, have navigated the complexities of human cognition. Their work has illuminated the intricate mechanisms that underpin memory, galvanizing knowledge that inspires contemporary strategies in memory enhancement while establishing a framework for future exploration. Through this legacy, we grasp the monumental importance memory holds—not just as a performative aspect of cognition, but as a vital element of human experience, understanding, and innovation. As we stand at the precipice of tomorrow's cognitive enhancement landscape, the insights gleaned from the past broaden our horizons, inviting us to continue to push the boundaries of what is possible in the realm of memory and intelligence.

10.5. Constructing Tomorrow's Reality

In our rapidly evolving world of cognitive enhancement and memory techniques, the endeavor to construct tomorrow's reality through innovative methods can be understood by exploring the historical context, the latest scientific advancements, and the profound impact that these techniques have on human memory and cognition. This examination highlights the critical role that structured memory techniques like memory palaces play not only in personal cognitive development but also in shaping societal perceptions of intelligence, learning, and technology integration.

The narrative begins with our historical understanding of memory. Ancient civilizations crafted intricate mnemonic techniques, such as the Method of Loci, which laid the foundation for our modern approaches to memory enhancement. These early memory techniques were more than simple tools; they reflected the human desire for knowledge and understanding—a desire that persists today. Memory palaces, originally conceived as spaces where information is anchored to physical locations, provide a unique intersection where experiential learning meets imaginative cognitive architecture.

As we advance into the 21st century, the intersection of memory enhancement techniques and technological innovation presents unprecedented opportunities. Cutting-edge neuroscience has unveiled insights into how the brain encodes and retrieves memories, illuminating pathways that can be augmented by modern techniques. Research on neuroplasticity underscores that the brain's ability to adapt and grow is crucial to maximizing memory capabilities. Techniques that engage the brain in active memory construction—such as memory palaces—can, therefore, not only enhance retention but also foster cognitive flexibility.

Moreover, the integration of digital technology brings forth innovative tools that amplify our memory capabilities. Digital memory aids, interactive learning platforms, and AI-driven applications allow individuals to personalize and optimize their cognitive strategies. By utilizing artificial intelligence to adapt environments and suggest memory techniques tailored to individual needs, we see a shift towards personalized learning experiences that could significantly improve educational outcomes and cognitive skills.

The future reality emerges as we recognize that memory enhancement extends beyond mere retention; it fosters creativity, emotional engagement, and problem-solving abilities. Memory palaces and similar techniques encourage individuals to think divergently, crafting connections between disparate concepts and crafting narratives that instill deeper understanding. As we harness these capabilities, creativity flourishes, opening new avenues for innovation within personal and professional domains.

However, as we engage with these advancements, it is crucial to consider the ethical implications of cognitive enhancement. As the boundaries between human cognition and machine intelligence continue to blur, we must grapple with questions surrounding autonomy, privacy, and societal impact. The integration of memory technology challenges us to redefine what it means to learn and remember, prompting discussions about equitable access to these advancements and the potential consequences of over-reliance on technology for cognitive processes.

In this context, the construction of tomorrow's reality involves a proactive approach to memory enhancement. This includes advocating for diverse learning experiences that leverage memory techniques in educational settings, fostering environments where creativity thrives, and ensuring ethical standards are upheld as we incorporate technology into cognitive practices.

As we envision this integrated future, it becomes increasingly clear that memory enhancement is not merely about improving individual recall but represents a collective journey toward heightened intelligence and human flourishing. By constructing tomorrow's reality with an unwavering commitment to cognitive enhancement, we pave the way for a deeper appreciation of memory's role in shaping our identities, enriching our lives, and fostering a more connected and intelligent society.

Through structured techniques that bridge ancient wisdom with modern knowledge, we unlock the potential of human memory, ensuring that as we navigate an increasingly complex future, we remain equipped with the tools necessary to thrive and innovate in a world abundant with information. This journey toward memory mastery becomes an empowering quest, one that embraces the power of imagination and innovation while acknowledging the ethical landscape that guides our evolution as both learners and creators. By doing so, we honor the legacy of the past and boldly step into an empowered future where memory enhances both individual lives and the broader human experience.

11. The Role of Education and Brain Development

11.1. Linking Memory Development with Education

Memory serves as a cornerstone of educational development, directly influencing how individuals learn, retain, and apply knowledge throughout their lives. The foundations of memory development are critical not just for academic success but for personal growth and cognitive evolution. Acknowledging the powerful link between memory development and educational methodologies is essential for creating effective learning environments that resonate with learners of all ages.

At the core of this understanding is the realization that memory is not a static faculty; rather, it is a dynamic process intricately tied to the experiences and environments in which people learn. Informed by cognitive science, educators are beginning to apply principles that focus on enhancing memory through structured learning environments. Techniques such as spaced repetition, active learning, and the use of mnemonic devices invigorate traditional educational approaches by fostering deeper cognitive engagement and retention.

This correlation between formal education and memory structuring is particularly relevant as learners encounter increasingly complex content. The methodologies that promote optimal memory encoding and retrieval are critical for effective learning. For instance, implementing mnemonic devices like memory palaces encourages students to visualize information spatially, enhancing both retention and recall. This approach recognizes that memory operates through associative networks—making it possible to navigate vast amounts of information by anchoring knowledge to familiar concepts and experiences.

Moreover, the integration of auditory, visual, and kinesthetic learning styles into the curriculum further emphasizes the significance of memory development. Research suggests that engaging multiple senses during the learning process enhances retention and comprehension. Educational frameworks that accommodate diverse learning preferences enable learners to construct their own unique memory strategies, making cognitive connections that resonate with their individual experiences.

In addition to fostering an environment conducive to memory development, educational practitioners can leverage cutting-edge technology to enhance cognitive engagement. Digital tools and online platforms can support memory augmentation through interactive content and instant feedback that help learners apply their knowledge more effectively. When these digital methods are supported by a comprehensive understanding of memory principles, they prepare students to manage and apply information in practical contexts.

Furthermore, memory development must begin at an early age. The crucial early childhood years serve as the foundation for lifelong learning habits, making it imperative to implement memory-enhancing techniques during these formative stages. Programs that introduce children to mnemonic devices, storytelling, and visual learning can significantly impact their cognitive abilities and equip them with essential skills for future academic pursuits. Early engagement with memory strategies lays the groundwork for successful learning trajectories, fostering a love of knowledge that lasts a lifetime.

In educational settings, addressing disparities in learning is also essential for optimizing memory development. Strategic memory training initiatives can bridge gaps in access to quality education, empowering students from diverse backgrounds to develop effective cognitive skills. By tailoring memory techniques to accommodate different learning styles and cultural contexts, educators can ensure that memory development is inclusive and equitable, fostering environments where all learners can thrive.

Finally, the integration of holistic educational approaches that prioritize both cognitive and emotional development can further enhance memory capacity. Understanding that emotions significantly influence memory encoding, curricula designed with an emotional intelligence framework create supportive atmospheres conducive to learning. Such curricula encourage students to build connections with the material, making memory not just a retrieval task but a deeply personal engagement with knowledge.

In summary, linking memory development with education is not merely an academic exercise; it is a fundamental principle that shapes learning experiences. By adopting memory-enhancing techniques and leveraging technology, educators can create environments where learners feel empowered to explore and retain knowledge. Furthermore, early initiatives, addressing educational disparities, and fostering emotional engagement support the holistic development of memory capacity across diverse populations. As we continue to explore the intersections of memory and education, the aim must be to construct robust frameworks that nurture learners' cognitive potential and prepare them for lifelong success.

11.2. Early Development and Memory Initiatives

In the current educational landscape, the integration of early memory development initiatives holds immense potential for enhancing students' cognitive abilities and enriching their learning experiences. Fostering memory skills from a young age can have profound effects on academic performance, social interactions, and lifelong learning habits. Understanding how memory techniques can be effectively implemented during childhood is paramount for educators and parents alike, as it lays the groundwork for future cognitive success.

Memory techniques aimed at early education need to be adaptable, engaging, and sensitive to the developmental stages of children. First and foremost, employing playful and imaginative methods to teach memory techniques is essential. Children naturally thrive in environments that encourage creativity and expression, making storytelling an effective tool for memory development. Educators can use narratives that incorporate characters, adventures, and meaningful emotional connections, which help embed facts into memorable stories. By intertwining factual information with engaging narratives, children are more likely to retain what they have learned.

Additionally, the use of visual aids and multi-sensory approaches offers significant advantages in memory enhancement for young learners. Integrating visual elements, such as picture cards, diagrams, and posters within the learning environment, can strengthen associations and encourage recall. Memory palaces can be simplified for young children by guiding them to visualize familiar spaces—like their homes or classrooms—where they can place information they need to remember. At this level, the palace can consist of simple rooms that represent different subjects, colors, or themes, giving children a relatable framework for organizing their knowledge.

Incorporating games and activities that emphasize memory challenges further enhances cognitive development. Memory games, such as matching pairs or sequencing activities, provide playful contexts within which children can practice retaining and recalling information. Interactive exercises can include scavenger hunts where children must remember a list of items, engaging both their memory and sense of adventure. These enjoyable practices reinforce learning without the pressure often associated with traditional educational methodologies.

Furthermore, the development of routine and consistency is highly beneficial for memory retention in early learners. Children thrive in structured environments, and establishing consistent times for memory practice, such as daily storytelling sessions or memory game hours, can help foster long-term memory skills. Consistency cultivates a sense of security, allowing young learners to engage with memory techniques confidently and develop the capacity to remember information over time.

Furthermore, educators should closely monitor children's progress and adapt techniques based on their unique needs. Frequent assessments should be implemented to gauge which methods resonate with individual learners. By closely observing students' responses and retention rates, educators can tailor memory strategies to better suit the varying cognitive profiles of their students. This adaptability fosters individualized learning paths that encourage growth and improve overall memory capabilities.

Family involvement in early memory initiatives cannot be understated. When parents consciously engage with their children's memory development strategies at home, this reinforcement can enhance learning experiences significantly. Activities such as storytelling, mnemonic games, and sensory-rich experiences at home can solidify the techniques taught in school, promoting an environment that values memory as a vital cognitive skill. Building a collaborative approach reinforces memory development and fosters supportive relationships built on shared learning experiences.

In addition to these practical techniques, fostering a culture that celebrates curiosity, exploration, and self-discovery is crucial for encouraging children's memory development. Encouraging questions, exploration, and creative problem-solving nurtures a growth mindset that leads to cognitive flexibility. Children are more likely to adapt to memory techniques and engage deeply with the information when they feel empowered to explore their interests.

In summary, integrating early memory development initiatives into educational practices can transform the trajectory of children's cognitive abilities. By utilizing creative storytelling, visual aids, playful activities, routine practices, adaptability, parental involvement, and fostering a culture of curiosity, educators and parents can create enriching environments that promote strong memory skills. These foundational practices will nurture a lifelong passion for learning and equip children with the tools they need to tackle academic challenges with confidence. As we recognize the importance of early memory initiatives, we pave the way for intelligent, adaptive, and innovative future generations.

11.3. Addressing Educational Disparities

Addressing educational disparities is a multifaceted endeavor that employs strategic memory training as a vital tool in fostering accessible learning experiences for all students. As we have seen, the interplay between memory techniques, cognitive development, and educational practices has significant implications for promoting equity in education. By recognizing and addressing disparities in access to resources, learning environments, and instructional techniques, we can create systemic changes that empower every learner to reach their potential.

First and foremost, understanding the significance of memory in education is crucial for addressing disparities. Memory plays a central role in how we learn, retain, and apply knowledge. By employing techniques that enhance memory retention, such as memory palaces and spaced repetition, educators can provide all students with concrete strategies to improve their academic performance. These techniques can help bridge gaps in knowledge and foster a greater sense of agency among students who may feel overwhelmed by traditional rote memorization methods.

Implementing these memory enhancement techniques also requires thoughtful consideration of diverse learning needs. Students come to the classroom with varied backgrounds, experiences, and cognitive profiles that impact their educational journeys. For learners who face challenges, whether due to socioeconomic factors, language barriers, or learning differences, tailored memory strategies can provide crucial support. For instance, educators can design inclusive memory activities that allow students to contribute unique perspectives and experiences, facilitating an environment where all voices are valued. Collaborative learning models further emphasize peer-to-peer engagement, creating opportunities for students to learn from one another's strengths.

Additionally, leveraging technology as a means of addressing educational disparities offers tremendous potential for reaching underrepresented populations. With the advent of digital learning platforms and resources, educators can integrate memory training applications into their instructional practices, ensuring that students have access to tools that enhance their cognitive capabilities. By providing access to personalized memory training software, educators can help students optimize their learning processes, regardless of the barriers they may face. Through guided practice and interactive content, students can develop a sense of competency and confidence in their abilities to retain and recall information.

Moreover, community engagement plays a critical role in addressing educational disparities through memory training initiatives. Schools, local organizations, and families can collaborate to provide workshops or training programs that focus on memory enhancement for students and their families. Establishing a culture of learning that extends beyond the classroom helps reinforce the importance of memory techniques among students, parents, and educators alike. Creating resource-sharing networks within communities empowers individuals to access memory training resources and fosters a sense of collective ownership over educational development.

Finally, rigorous assessment and evaluation of memory development interventions are necessary to ensure that they effectively address disparities in educational outcomes. Collecting data on student performance, retention rates, and engagement levels helps educators identify which memory techniques are most effective in promoting learning for diverse populations. Continuous feedback loops enable educators to refine their instructional practices, ensuring that they remain responsive to students' evolving needs.

In conclusion, addressing educational disparities through strategic memory training requires a holistic approach built on the principles of inclusivity, adaptability, and collaboration. Enhancing memory retention not only equips students with essential skills for academic success but also fosters a sense of ownership and agency in their learning journeys. By leveraging technology, engaging communities, and implementing tailored strategies, educators can create equitable learning environments that empower all students to thrive. As we continue to explore the intersections of memory, equity, and education, our actions must be guided by a commitment to ensure that every learner has access to the cognitive tools necessary for achieving their fullest potential.

11.4. Holistic Educational Approaches

Holistic educational approaches encompass a comprehensive view of learning that integrates cognitive, emotional, social, and physical factors to optimize memory retention and cognitive performance. As the landscape of education evolves, recognizing the importance of approaching memory enhancement holistically becomes essential for fostering well-rounded learners who are equipped to navigate the complexities of modern life.

At the core of holistic education is the understanding that each learner is unique, shaped by diverse backgrounds, experiences, and needs. Traditional educational methods often prioritize rote memorization and standardized assessment, which may fail to accommodate the multi-faceted nature of human cognition. In holistic approaches, this narrow view is expanded to consider how to effectively engage students across various dimensions—intellectually, emotionally, socially, and physically—to create an enriching learning environment.

Central to these holistic educational approaches is the integration of cognitive development techniques that emphasize memory and engagement. Techniques such as the Method of Loci, visualization, and storytelling transform how learners interact with information. Memory palaces, for instance, invite students to visualize their learning spaces as interactive environments filled with vivid images and stories, allowing them to anchor information in a personal context. These methods not only enhance memory retention but also promote creativity and critical thinking.

Additionally, the promotion of emotional intelligence within the educational framework is invaluable for fostering interconnectedness between emotional well-being and cognitive processes. By encouraging self-awareness, empathy, and interpersonal skills, holistic approaches create a supportive atmosphere that enhances learning outcomes. When students feel valued and understood, their motivation to engage in the learning process increases, thereby augmenting their capacity to retain and recall information.

The inclusion of social learning experiences is another vital component of holistic educational approaches. Collaborative group activities, peer-to-peer learning, and project-based initiatives not only nurture communication and teamwork skills but also enrich memory through shared experiences. When learners discuss and explore concepts together, they create stronger associative networks that reinforce their understanding of the material. Engaging in dialogue allows different perspectives to emerge, deepening cognitive connections and enhancing the quality of learning.

Physical well-being also plays an important role in holistic education. Research has shown that regular physical activity is positively correlated with cognitive performance, including memory retention. By incorporating movement into the learning environment—whether through physical education, brain breaks, or mindfulness practices —educators can support the cognitive development of students. Techniques that facilitate mindfulness and focus help students remain engaged and avoid cognitive overload, ultimately fostering healthier learning environments.

Furthermore, integrating brain exercises into the curriculum enhances cognitive functions and memory development. Activities that promote critical thinking, problem-solving, and creativity challenge learners to engage with information meaningfully. By prioritizing cognitive exercises alongside traditional learning materials, educators can foster a dynamic and interactive learning atmosphere.

Holistic educational approaches are particularly beneficial in addressing diverse learning needs and supporting students who may struggle with traditional methods. Tailoring memory techniques to accommodate various learning styles ensures that all students, regardless of their backgrounds or cognitive profiles, can access the tools necessary to succeed.

Finally, collaboration among educators, parents, and communities reinforces holistic educational practices. Engaging families and community members in the learning process enriches the educational experience and encourages a culture of continuous learning. By creating partnerships that support memory development initiatives, we can establish learning environments that extend beyond the classroom walls.

In conclusion, holistic educational approaches represent a comprehensive framework for memory development that emphasizes the interplay between cognitive, emotional, social, and physical aspects of learning. By integrating diverse memory techniques, emotional intelligence, collaborative experiences, and physical well-being into educational practices, we cultivate a deeper understanding of the multidimensional nature of learning. These approaches not only enhance memory retention but also create a supportive and engaging atmosphere that empowers learners to thrive academically and personally. Through a dedication to holistic education, we lay the groundwork for a future where individuals are equipped with the cognitive tools necessary to navigate an increasingly complex world.

11.5. Brain Exercises and Supportive Curriculum

In the quest for academic success and cognitive enhancement, innovative curricula integrating brain exercises and supportive learning methods play a crucial role. By focusing on the intricate relationship between memory development and effective learning strategies, educational institutions can empower students to reach their potential. Research has shown that a strong foundation in memory techniques enhances retention, comprehension, and the application of knowledge across disciplines. The following detailed exploration highlights how structured curriculum designs can harness brain exercises to optimize memory retention and foster holistic cognitive development.

Brain exercises serve as a fundamental component of a comprehensive approach to learning, enhancing both memory capacity and cognitive agility. Incorporating neural pathways training—such as memory games, puzzles, and spatial reasoning tasks—enables students to engage actively with content. Educators can incorporate these exercises into their lesson plans to create an engaging atmosphere conducive to learning. For example, students could participate in short memory challenges at the start of each class. Such activities not only warm up cognitive functions but also create a dynamic entry point for deeper exploration of subject material.

Beyond traditional approaches, incorporating technology into brain exercises opens new avenues for memory enhancement. Digital platforms and applications allow students to engage with interactive content, reinforcing concepts through gamification. Mobile apps designed for memory training, such as flashcard systems or spaced repetition tools, can be integrated into the curriculum to provide students with ongoing practice opportunities beyond the classroom. These modern tools make learning continuous and immersive, catering to contemporary expectations while sustaining motivation.

Furthermore, collaborative learning techniques bolster memory retention and enrich the educational landscape. Structuring group activities, peer-to-peer memory-sharing exercises, and cooperative projects fosters peer interactions that enhance retention. Research highlights that discussing and explaining material to fellow students can reinforce understanding and increase recall. Collaborating allows students to benefit from diverse perspectives, adding depth to their learning experiences.

Integrating memory techniques into a curriculum does not solely enhance retention but also encourages creativity and critical thinking. Students engaged in active memory strategies are prompted to think creatively about how to connect ideas and concepts. For instance, utilizing memory palaces allows learners to visualize information within an imaginative framework, promoting cognitive flexibility.

This creative approach can transform rote learning into an interactive exercise—sparking enthusiasm for the subject matter.

Inclusivity is another essential consideration in developing curricula centered around brain exercises. By recognizing the diverse learning styles and cognitive profiles present in a classroom, educators can design memory strategies that accommodate all students. Implementing various techniques—from visual aids to auditory cues and tactile experiences—ensures that memory enhancement efforts resonate with each individual. Creating a supportive environment where all students feel valued fosters a sense of belonging, further enhancing learning outcomes.

Moreover, memory-focused curricula can actively promote a growth mindset, guiding learners to see challenges as opportunities for improvement rather than obstacles. By reinforcing that memory skills can be cultivated over time and through consistent practice, students are motivated to embrace their learning journeys. Educators can use language and messaging that emphasizes the iterative nature of learning, framing brain exercises as essential building blocks on the path to mastery.

The impact of brain exercises and supportive curricula extends beyond academics into lifelong learning. Students equipped with effective memory techniques are better prepared to navigate future challenges, whether in their careers or personal pursuits. As cognitive enhancement becomes increasingly integral to modern education, it's vital to prioritize memory development as a foundational aspect of intellectual growth.

In conclusion, merging brain exercises with supportive curricula constitutes a holistic approach that paves the way for academic excellence and cognitive agility. By emphasizing interactive, imaginative, and inclusive strategies, educational institutions can empower students to develop essential memory skills. The aim is not merely to memorize facts but to cultivate an adaptive, resilient, and engaged mindset toward learning that encourages curiosity, creativity, and a lifelong pursuit of knowledge. Through this integrated model, we unlock students' cognitive potential, preparing them for future success in a complex and ever-changing world.

12. Digital Memory: Lifelong Learning Platforms

12.1. Online Learning and Cognitive Retention

As the digital landscape continues to evolve, the interplay between online learning and cognitive retention garners increasing attention as an essential component of contemporary education. With countless resources and tools available for enhancing memory, it is vital to explore how these online environments facilitate cognitive processes and promote knowledge acquisition. This exploration emphasizes the importance of structure, engagement, and personalization in maximizing memory retention within digital platforms, ultimately empowering learners to navigate the vast information landscape of the digital age effectively.

At the core of successful online learning lies the fundamental principle of active engagement with the material. Research consistently supports the notion that learners retain information better when involved actively in the learning process. Online environments provide a unique opportunity to harness various interactive techniques, transforming passive learning into dynamic experiences. Employing methods such as gamification, interactive quizzes, and multimedia presentations not only enriches the learning experience but also serves to stimulate cognitive pathways that facilitate memory retention.

Furthermore, many online learning platforms utilize spaced repetition algorithms to optimize review schedules. Spaced repetition takes advantage of the forgetting curve, reinforcing previously learned concepts just as individuals are about to forget them. The use of digital platforms allows for efficient tracking of progress and personalization of review intervals, making it easier for learners to engage consistently with the material over time. This systematic approach to reinforcement can significantly enhance long-term retention, as it aligns with the principles of cognitive psychology that emphasize the importance of distributed practice.

Personalization is another key factor in maximizing cognitive retention in online learning. The role of adaptive learning technologies that tailor the educational experience to individual preferences and abilities cannot be overstated. Personalized learning pathways allow students to choose topics relevant to their interests, accommodating various cognitive styles while fostering intrinsic motivation. Memory techniques, such as the Method of Loci, can be integrated into these platforms, enabling learners to create mental palaces tailored to their specific content using familiar contexts and imagery that resonate with them. This personalized approach not only heightens emotional engagement but also fortifies memory connections, making retention more effective.

Additionally, the inherent collaborative nature of online learning fosters peer-to-peer interactions that can enhance cognitive retention. It is well established that discussing material with others reinforces knowledge and promotes deeper understanding. Collaborative platforms, forums, and discussion boards provide spaces for learners to share insights, ask questions, and build connections, creating a supportive learning ecosystem. As learners articulate their understanding and share their memory strategies, they enhance both their own retention and that of their peers, leading to a richer collective cognitive experience.

Massive Open Online Courses (MOOCs) represent a significant innovation in online learning that demonstrates the potential for memory enhancement at scale. These MOOCs often offer structured curricula developed by experts, blending diverse methods of content delivery, including video lectures, readings, assignments, and interactive assessments. Learners from varied backgrounds can access high-quality content, allowing for widespread knowledge retention. Moreover, the flexibility of MOOCs provides the opportunity for learners to engage with the material at their own pace, facilitating deeper cognitive processing—a crucial aspect of memory retention.

In envisioning the future of online learning and cognitive retention, the integration of emerging technologies such as virtual reality (VR) and artificial intelligence (AI) holds great promise. VR can create immersive learning environments that facilitate experiential learning and deep engagement, while AI can analyze individual learning patterns, offering personalized memory techniques tailored to enhance retention. As technology continues to evolve, the digital classroom will further transform, fostering immersive experiences that optimize the learning process and improve cognitive outcomes.

In summary, the synergy between online learning and cognitive retention is underscored by active engagement, personalization, collaboration, and the use of memory enhancement techniques. Through innovative platforms and adaptive technologies, learners can access an array of resources designed to enrich their educational experiences while fostering meaningful memory connections. The transformative potential of online learning environments empowers individuals to navigate the complexities of the digital age, effectively enhancing their cognitive retention and promoting lifelong learning. As we move forward, the emphasis on optimizing memory within online learning contexts will be vital in shaping future educational practices that resonate with the needs and aspirations of learners around the globe.

12.2. Apps and Tools for Memory Enhancement

As we step into the realm of memory enhancement, it's crucial to explore the modern tools and applications that complement age-old techniques. In today's digital age, a variety of applications and tools have emerged, promising to assist individuals in enhancing their memory capabilities. These tools leverage principles from cognitive science and offer innovative techniques that can be applied in everyday learning and memory retention.

One of the most notable developments in the field of memory enhancement is the rise of mobile applications that integrate memory techniques into user-friendly systems. These apps often use methods like spaced repetition, which has been scientifically proven to improve memory retention by reintroducing information at strategically timed intervals. Users can input custom flashcards or select predefined sets of information, allowing for a personalized learning experience tailored to their unique needs. Platforms such as Anki and Quizlet have harnessed this principle, offering engaging interfaces where learners can practice and reinforce their memory skills with ease.

Another key innovation is the emergence of digital memory palaces. Several apps, such as "Memrise" and "Memory Palace," allow users to create vivid, imaginative memory landscapes that they can navigate mentally. Within these spaces, users can store information in a way that aligns with their existing knowledge and spatial reasoning. This integration of traditional mnemonic techniques with modern technology enhances cognitive engagement, making the process of memorization not just effective but also enjoyable. By creating unique imagery associated with specific information, users can facilitate deeper encoding and easier recall.

The integration of gamification into memory enhancement tools adds another layer of engagement. By turning memory practice into games or interactive challenges, users are motivated to participate regularly and enthusiastically. Apps like "Elevate" and "Lumosity" not only provide cognitive training exercises but do so in a manner that resembles gameplay, leading to higher levels of user engagement and sustained practice. This approach aligns with our understanding of motivation and learning: when users find enjoyment in the learning process, they are more likely to stick with memory-enhancing activities and see real improvements.

Furthermore, the potential of augmented reality (AR) and virtual reality (VR) in memory enhancement is generating excitement in educational contexts. These immersive technologies allow learners to create more interactive memory palaces where they can visualize and interact with information in 3D environments. Initiatives exploring VR for educational purposes, like "Oculus Education," promise to elevate traditional learning experiences into spatial engagements, making the material more memorable. The combination of depth, sensory involvement, and interactivity can lead to more robust memory formation.

The popularity of podcasts and audio content also presents unique opportunities for auditory memory retention. Audio learning taps into an alternative memory modality that complements visual learning by engaging learners in a different way. Platforms such as "Audible" or "Podcast Addict" make it possible for users to consume information on-the-go while strengthening auditory recall, thereby broadening their cognitive toolkit.

As with any field, research and development in memory enhancement tools necessitate ethical considerations surrounding data privacy, accessibility, and inclusivity. It's vital that developers prioritize user privacy, ensuring that personal data utilized for memory enhancement is handled with care. Moreover, accessibility to these tools must be a primary consideration, as technology should serve as an equalizer rather than a divider. Expanding outreach and resources for individuals from all backgrounds can help democratize access to high-quality cognitive tools and training.

In conclusion, the modern apps and tools dedicated to memory enhancement represent a synthesis of cognitive science, technology, and age-old mnemonic techniques. By employing spaced repetition, gamification, memory palaces, and immersive technologies, learners are empowered to optimize their memory potential and foster deeper engagement with information. As these tools continue to evolve, they will undoubtedly play a critical role in shaping how we learn, remember, and interact with knowledge in our increasingly digital world.

12.3. Collaborative Learning Techniques

In today's world, where rapid advancements in technology continually reshape our lives, the significance of collaborative learning techniques emerges as a cornerstone for effective knowledge acquisition and memory retention. Collaborative learning is predicated on the idea that individuals learn best when they engage with one another, sharing experiences and insights that enrich their understanding of the material. By harnessing the power of social interaction and peer-supported learning, collaborative techniques can significantly enhance memory performance, foster creativity, and prepare individuals for the complexities of an interconnected world.

At the heart of collaborative learning is the acknowledgment that learning is inherently social. Humans are social beings by nature, and through collaboration, we create a dynamic environment where diverse perspectives and experiences coalesce. This interaction lays the groundwork for meaningful discussions and deeper conceptual understanding, ultimately leading to improved memory retention. When learners explain concepts to their peers or engage in dialogue that challenges their thoughts, they strengthen their understanding. This process not only promotes recall but also enhances the ability to connect ideas, facilitating deeper cognitive processing.

One of the key techniques in collaborative learning is cooperative group work. By working in small groups, learners can tackle complex problems together, benefiting from the shared responsibility and diverse skills of each member. Within this setting, individuals can take on different roles, such as note-taker, presenter, or researcher, allowing for a rich exchange of ideas. Each participant brings their own background knowledge and insights, creating a more robust learning experience that leads to improved memory encoding and retrieval. For example, when students collaborate on a group project, they engage in discussions, explore various approaches, and outline findings collectively, solidifying their understanding through mutual reinforcement and shared memory cues.

Another avenue for enhancing collaborative learning techniques lies in technology. Online learning platforms, virtual classrooms, and communication tools foster collaborative environments, even when physical proximity is absent. These platforms provide opportunities for asynchronous discussions, enabling learners to engage with one another at their own pace while benefiting from the richness of peer exchange. For instance, discussion forums and collaborative tools like

Google Docs allow learners to form dynamic study groups and share resources, enriching the engagement with the material. By utilizing technology to facilitate collaborative learning, students are better equipped to access a wealth of insights, enhancing their memory retention through shared experiences and interactions.

Moreover, the integration of collaborative learning techniques within educational curricula can have lasting effects on cognitive development. The ability to engage in teamwork and group discussions cultivates essential skills beyond academic knowledge, including communication, critical thinking, and emotional intelligence. As learners navigate group dynamics, they develop essential life skills that translate to real-world contexts, fostering successful interpersonal relationships in their personal and professional lives. The shared experiences that arise from collaborative learning create a social fabric of memory, where individuals build connections that extend beyond the classroom.

However, collaborative learning is not without its challenges. Factors such as group dynamics, varying levels of engagement, or differential contributions from group members can affect the overall effectiveness of the learning experience. It is crucial for educators and facilitators to implement strategies that promote inclusive participation and equitable distribution of responsibilities. Encouraging group norms that prioritize accountability and respectful communication can mitigate these challenges, ensuring that collaborative learning remains productive and enriching for all participants.

Furthermore, fostering an environment where making mistakes is viewed as a learning opportunity is key to enhancing memory through collaboration. When individuals feel comfortable taking risks, they are more likely to experiment with ideas and engage deeply with the material. This atmosphere of psychological safety encourages learners to share insights and questions openly, reinforcing memory through peer support and encouragement.

In summary, collaborative learning techniques are invaluable tools for enhancing memory retention and cognitive performance. By embracing the social nature of learning, utilizing technology to facilitate interaction, and implementing strategies to address potential challenges, educators and learners can create environments that empower individuals to explore knowledge together. These collaborative experiences not only enrich our understanding of complex material but also foster the social skills and emotional intelligence that play vital roles in navigation through an increasingly interconnected world. Ultimately, the path ahead should embrace the spirit of collaboration as a means for collective cognitive growth, guiding learners toward a future where they not only remember better but engage more meaningfully with knowledge and each other.

12.4. MOOCs and Memory Mastery

In the age of digital intelligence, understanding the potential of Massive Open Online Courses (MOOCs) in enhancing memory mastery has become increasingly relevant. MOOCs have revolutionized the landscape of education by providing learners from diverse backgrounds with access to high-quality content, fostering an environment that amplifies memory retention and cognitive enhancement. By incorporating structured techniques in memory training, MOOCs engage learners in ways that align with current research on effective memory enhancement strategies.

The first overarching theme contributing to memory mastery within MOOCs is the emphasis on active engagement. Research consistently reveals that learners who are actively involved in their educational experiences retain information more effectively than those who passively consume content. MOOCs facilitate this active engagement by incorporating interactive elements, such as quizzes, discussion forums, and peer review processes, that prompt learners to articulate their understanding and apply new concepts. For instance, after a lecture on a complex topic, a follow-up quiz encourages participants to recall key information, reinforcing memory through immediate application. This continuous interaction not only solidifies knowledge but also fosters a greater sense of ownership as learners navigate their memory-enhancing journeys.

Another factor that contributes to memory mastery through MOOCs is the structured use of spaced repetition. Research in cognitive psychology shows that information is better retained when it is revisited at strategically spaced intervals. Many MOOCs integrate this principle by providing regular review sessions and quizzes at varying points throughout a course duration, ensuring that learners engage with material consistently over time. This approach aligns with the forgetting curve, allowing users to reinforce their memory pathways effectively. By actively revisiting learned content rather than cramming, learners can better retain information long-term—a crucial component of effective memory practices.

The flexibility inherent in MOOCs further enhances memory mastery by allowing learners to curate their learning experiences to suit their individual learning preferences. Participants have the autonomy to choose specific modules or topics based on their interests, thereby ensuring more meaningful engagement with the material. This personalization resonates with principles of motivation in memory enhancement, as learners are more likely to focus on content that they find relevant and engaging. Consequently, this targeted approach leads to a deeper cognitive connection with the subject matter, promoting retention and mastery.

Moreover, the collaborative learning potential presented by MOOCs bolsters memory enhancement. Many platforms foster community interactions where learners can engage with peers, share insights, and discuss concepts. This dialogue not only enriches understanding but also facilitates collective memory processes, where knowledge becomes socially constructed. Memory retention deepens through social interaction, as discussing and explaining concepts to others reinforces individual understanding. MOOCs thus provide an accessible avenue for learners to establish partnerships and networks, extending their memory mastery through meaningful collaboration.

The incorporation of multimedia elements offers additional advantages to memory enhancement within MOOCs. Visual aids, instructional videos, and interactive simulations cater to diverse learning styles, promoting engagement across various cognitive approaches. Visualizations are particularly effective, as they facilitate memory encoding by attaching information to memorable images, diagrams, or animations. By appealing to different sensory modalities, MOOCs ensure that learners have multiple avenues for memory retrieval, thus boosting overall cognitive retention.

As we consider future directions, the evolution of MOOCs presents opportunities to integrate emerging technologies such as Artificial Intelligence (AI) and data analytics to optimize learning experiences. Personalized learning platforms can utilize data-driven insights to adapt course content to individual learners' needs and memory-enhancing techniques. These advancements will not only foster enhanced cognitive engagement but also ensure that memory practices resonate with contemporary learners in dynamic ways.

In summary, MOOCs have emerged as a powerful mechanism for mastering memory through active engagement, structured review processes, personalized learning experiences, collaborative interactions, and diverse multimedia resources. By embracing these principles, learners can foster a robust memory foundation that enhances retention while enabling them to thrive in an increasingly complex world. As MOOCs continue to evolve and integrate innovative approaches to memory mastery, they hold the potential to shape a future where cognitive enhancement becomes an intrinsic element of the learning journey.

12.5. Future Directions of Digital Memory Initiatives

As we stand on the precipice of a new era in memory and cognitive enhancement, the future directions of digital memory initiatives promise a transformative landscape that intertwines technology with the art of remembering. The expansion of digital engagement in cognitive growth reveals not only the profound potential to enhance personal memory capabilities but also the ways in which broader societal shifts will unfold as we integrate these tools into our daily lives.

The journey into this future begins with recognizing the role of digital tools in reshaping how individuals interact with information. As technology continues to evolve at an unprecedented pace, the potential for apps, platforms, and online learning environments designed to enhance memory expands dramatically. By harnessing the principles of cognitive science, these digital initiatives aim to build personalized learning experiences that accommodate diverse learning styles, boost engagement, and optimize retention. From interactive memory games to customized flashcard systems, the future will see a proliferation of refined tools that cater to individual cognitive profiles, transforming the landscape of memory enhancement into a tailored experience.

Moreover, as we explore digital memory initiatives, we cannot overlook the significance of social connectivity in the digital age. The online environment provides unique opportunities for collaborative learning, where individuals can engage with peers across the globe and share insights, strategies, and personal experiences. This community aspect fosters a collective pursuit of memory mastery, creating a culture that values shared knowledge and reinforces learning practices. As tools for virtual collaboration improve, we will likely see enhanced collective memory techniques that integrate digital resources with the power of social interaction, promoting higher retention levels and creativity through shared experiences.

In parallel, the advancement of artificial intelligence promises to revolutionize how memory is managed and utilized. AI algorithms can analyze individual learning behaviors, offering personalized memory strategies that adapt to changing needs. As these systems learn from users, they can provide targeted prompts, reminders, and adaptive learning experiences that optimize cognitive engagement. This synergy between human cognition and machine intelligence opens new doors for enhancing the capability to remember and retrieve information, transforming the way we approach memory training.

However, with these opportunities come the ethical considerations that should guide the development of digital memory initiatives. As memory enhancement tools become more integrated into our lives, discussions surrounding data privacy, autonomy, and the long-term implications of cognitive interventions will be critical. Ensuring that users maintain control over their cognitive data and experiences, while navigating these advancements responsibly, will be vital for fostering trust within the public sphere. Ethical frameworks surrounding cognitive enhancement must be established, guiding developers and users alike toward practices that prioritize well-being and social equity.

Furthermore, accessibility remains a pressing concern. As technology becomes a centerpiece of memory enhancement, addressing the digital divide will be essential to ensure that all individuals—regardless of socioeconomic status—can benefit from these advancements. Initiatives that promote equitable access to cognitive tools, education, and resources are imperative as we strive to create an inclusive approach to memory enhancement that empowers learners in every corner of society.

Ultimately, the future of digital memory initiatives rests not solely on the technologies themselves but on the collective intentionality with which we engage with these tools. By remaining mindful of the interplay between technology, memory, and human experience, we can cultivate a landscape that values memory enhancement as not just a means of cognitive improvement but as a path toward enriched learning and personal development.

As we imagine the horizon of memory and cognition, the synthesis of innovative technologies with individualized experiences creates a vivid tapestry of opportunities that await us. By embracing the transformational potential of digital memory initiatives, we will unlock new pathways for learning, understanding, and remembering

—which will significantly shape the way we experience knowledge in the world to come. Together, we stand at the brink of a future where memory is not merely preserved but augmented in daily life, leading to profound enhancements in our cognitive capabilities and the structure of human intelligence itself.

13. Ethical and Philosophical Considerations

13.1. The Ethics of Cognitive Enhancement

Memory enhancement and cognitive augmentation, particularly through memory palaces, thus raise a myriad of ethical considerations that warrant careful exploration. As we stand on the brink of a revolution wherein techniques to boost memory retention and cognitive function are increasingly accessible, it becomes imperative to address the implications of manipulating human cognition.

Consider the deeply personal aspects of memory: memories shape our identities, inform our decisions, and hold emotional significance. The power to enhance or alter these memories introduces profound ethical dilemmas. For instance, will individuals be truly informed about the potential consequences—both positive and negative—of memory augmentation? Cognitive enhancement methods, whether they involve traditional techniques like memory palaces or digital tools, must prioritize informed consent. Individuals should fully understand what they are embarking on, including how these techniques might reshape their cognitive landscape.

Furthermore, the prospect of cognitive enhancement raises questions regarding fairness and equity in access to such technologies. In an era where disparities in educational and cognitive development are pervasive, how can we ensure that access to memory enhancement techniques is equitable? Will learners from disadvantaged backgrounds be left behind, further exacerbating existing inequalities? It is vital to advocate for initiatives that democratize access to memory-enhancing tools, ensuring that all individuals, irrespective of socioeconomic status, can benefit from the potential advantages of cognitive augmentation.

Moreover, as cognitive enhancement technologies become more advanced, we must also be vigilant in considering the potential for dependency. The allure of technology as a memory aid is enticing, but will this create reliance on external devices at the expense of developing intrinsic cognitive skills? Just as the rise of calculators didn't eliminate the need for basic arithmetic understanding, the overuse of memory enhancement tools may risk creating a generation that fails to cultivate foundational cognitive strategies essential for problem-solving and critical thinking.

On a broader scale, societal implications must be examined. Integrating memory enhancement techniques into educational systems can foster an environment where learning becomes increasingly mechanized. This trend may foster cultures that prioritize memorization and cognitive prowess over creativity, emotional intelligence, and holistic learning experiences. We must ask ourselves: what kind of intelligence do we desire to cultivate? A narrow focus on cognitive enhancement should not distract from the importance of nurturing well-rounded individuals who are not only capable of recalling information but also proficient in developing relationships, solving problems, and adapting to new challenges.

In navigating these ethical and philosophical considerations, it is pivotal to engage in ongoing dialogues among educators, technologists, ethicists, and the wider community. These discussions will provide critical insight into how we can embrace the potential of cognitive enhancement responsibly while ensuring that human dignity, autonomy, and the diversity of experience remain at the forefront of our endeavors. Moreover, fostering interdisciplinary collaborations may reveal innovative solutions to address the ethical dilemmas associated with memory enhancement and cognitive augmentation.

In conclusion, as we venture into the era of cognitive enhancement, grappling with the ethical ramifications of memory manipulation is paramount. By fostering inclusive access, preserving the autonomy of the individual, and creating spaces for ethical deliberation, we can tap into the profound potential memory augmentation holds while honoring the complex tapestry of human experience. Through this collective effort, the pursuit of memory enhancement can ultimately enhance our understanding of what it means to be human, fostering an evolving balance between technology and cognition.

13.2. Philosophy of Human Cognition

The concept of human cognition is a rich tapestry woven with threads of philosophy, psychology, neuroscience, and culture. This intricate interplay shapes our understanding of how we think, learn, and remember. The evolving discourse surrounding cognition reflects not only our quest for knowledge but also our enduring curiosity about the fundamental nature of consciousness and the processes that underlie it.

From a philosophical standpoint, inquiries into the nature of consciousness suggest that human cognition is not merely a mechanical function of the brain. It invites exploration into subjective experiences, self-awareness, and metacognition—the ability to think about one's own thinking. These layers of cognitive engagement illustrate that the processes by which we remember, forget, and ultimately learn are intrinsically tied to our identity and the conscious experience of being human.

Memory plays a pivotal role in this philosophical domain, serving as a connection between past experiences and present actions. Philosophers such as John Locke have grappled with the implications of memory on personal identity, proposing that our memories shape who we are. The profound question posits: without memory, would we still exist as individuals? This exploration of identity invites consideration of memory's reliability and malleability, emphasizing that while it connects us to our histories, it may also distort our perceptions of the present.

Within cognitive science, advances in understanding the neural underpinnings of memory formation and retrieval have significantly influenced our perspectives on cognition. Neuroscientific research has unveiled the mechanisms of synaptic plasticity, highlighting how our experiences—both emotional and factual—forge connections within the brain. The interplay between the hippocampus and neocortex showcases how memories are encoded, consolidated, and retrieved, affirming that cognition is not an isolated process but rather a vast network of neural interactions.

Moreover, the influence of culture on human cognition cannot be understated. Our cognitive processes are shaped by the environments and contexts we inhabit, informing our beliefs, values, and memory techniques. The diverse ways in which societies value memory and learning unveil the cultural dimensions of cognition. For instance, collectivist cultures may emphasize communal storytelling and shared memory practices, while individualistic societies may prioritize personal achievement and individual recall methods. This cultural lens enhances our understanding of the multiplicity of cognitive experiences across the globe.

As we consider the future of human cognition, we find ourselves at a critical intersection—one that melds imagination and innovation while simultaneously grappling with ethical implications. The advent of cognitive enhancement technologies sparks debates on the essence of authenticity in memory and the right to cognitive integrity. As we navigate the landscapes of memory augmentation through digital technologies and cognitive tools, understanding the ramifications of these advancements requires a balance between innovation and individual rights.

Additionally, the philosophical discourse around intellectual fairness and memory enhancement unveils important questions about the implications of cognitive interventions on society. If cognitive enhancement technologies afford certain individuals an advantage, how do we ensure equitable access? The task of developing policies that promote openness and inclusivity in cognitive enhancement is paramount as we advance toward a future where memory and intelligence can be augmented.

Ultimately, the philosophy of human cognition invites us to embrace complexity—to celebrate the beauty of memory, identity, consciousness, and the multifaceted approaches that shape our understanding of intelligence. The tapestry of cognition, imbued with cultural, ethical, and philosophical reflections, beckons us toward a future that not only enhances memory and intelligence but fosters profound connections between our past, present, and anticipated futures. As we continue this journey, let us navigate the realm of human cognition with curiosity and intention, paving paths for exploration that intertwine with the essence of what it means to be human.

13.3. Balancing Innovation with Privacy

As technological advancements continue to shape our society, the balance between innovation and individual privacy remains a pressing issue, especially in the realm of cognitive enhancement and memory techniques. As tools designed to augment our memory capabilities, whether through memory palaces, digital applications, or neural interfaces, proliferate, it becomes crucial to consider the rights of individuals regarding their cognitive data. This challenge involves understanding how innovation can proceed without undermining personal privacy, securing the ethical integrity of cognitive enhancements while maximizing potential benefits.

With the advent of cognitive enhancement technologies, the instrumentality of personal data has entered the foreground. Much like medical records, cognitive data—comprising patterns of memory usage, preferred learning styles, and information retention scores—reflects deep insights into an individual's intellectual landscape. As educational institutions, corporations, and app developers gather this data to personalize cognitive enhancement experiences, safeguarding the privacy of learners must remain a primary concern. Thus, the ability of users to control their data—understand its use and implications, grant consent, and revoke access when desired—becomes essential in developing trust between users and cognitive technology providers.

However, the current landscape raises critical concerns regarding what constitutes informed consent in cognitive enhancement. Users may not fully comprehend the risks associated with densely interconnected technology and the implications of sharing personal cognitive data. This lack of understanding can lead to the unintended consequences of memory enhancement initiatives, where individual privacy is compromised, and users unwittingly become subjects of extensive profiling. Establishing transparent guidelines around cognitive data usage, consent protocols, and user rights is imperative for ensuring responsible innovation in cognitive technologies.

Furthermore, ethical frameworks must be developed to govern the use of artificial intelligence (AI) in analyzing and interpreting cognitive data. As AI systems become increasingly integrated into cognitive enhancement tools, questions emerge regarding accountability, bias, and accuracy in the data interpretation process. It is imperative to scrutinize how these systems are designed and maintained, ensuring that the algorithms do not exacerbate existing biases or misrepresent individual capabilities. The responsibility to develop equitable and ethical AI systems lies with developers and researchers, and an interdisciplinary approach combining ethicists, cognitive scientists, and technologists can help guide ethical considerations in cognitive enhancement.

The intersection of cognitive enhancement technologies and privacy also exposes broader societal implications. As innovations become mainstream, there's a risk of creating a divide between those who can afford enhanced cognitive tools and those who cannot. This disparity could lead to cognitive inequalities—where individuals with access to innovative cognitive enhancement tools navigate the knowledge economy with greater ease, while others are left behind. Thus, as society progresses toward cognitive enhancement, policies and initiatives should prioritize accessibility to these technologies, ensuring that innovations benefit all individuals, irrespective of their socioeconomic status.

As we reflect on the future, creating a culture that values both innovation and privacy will become integral to our approach to cognitive enhancement. Ongoing dialogues around privacy rights, ethical standards, and individual agency must be prioritized. Emphasizing educational initiatives that equip users with knowledge about the implications of cognitive enhancement technologies empowers users to make informed decisions regarding their personal data, ultimately strengthening the ethical core of innovations in this field.

In conclusion, the balance between innovation and privacy in cognitive enhancement presents multifaceted challenges requiring careful consideration. By championing informed consent, ethical governance, and equitable access, we can foster innovation that serves to enhance cognitive abilities without compromising individual rights. As we navigate this complex terrain, it is vital to actively engage stakeholders in discussions surrounding cognitive data and technology, ensuring that our journey into memory and intelligence augmentation remains rooted in ethical integrity and respect for individual privacy. Ultimately, the convergence of cognitive enhancement and privacy will shape a future where innovations amplify our cognitive potential while safeguarding the essence of human experience.

13.4. Philosophical Debates on Intellectual Fair Play

As society evolves, philosophical debates surrounding intellectual fairness gain prominence in the context of cognitive enhancements, particularly in an age where memory techniques and technologies offer unprecedented opportunities to augment our cognitive abilities. Significant discussions emerge regarding the implications and ethics of enhancing memory, intelligence, and cognitive performance through externally imposed methods. These debates explore notions of equity, accessibility, and the fundamental principles of what constitutes "fair play" in intellectual pursuits.

Central to the discourse on intellectual fairness is the recognition that not everyone has equal access to cognitive enhancement tools. Memory techniques such as mnemonic devices or cutting-edge technology like AI-assisted learning platforms may provide considerable advantages to those who can afford or access them. This disparity raises important questions about whether the use of such enhancements creates imbalanced competition—especially in educational and professional environments. Should success in these arenas be based not only on inherent intelligence or talent but also on the resources available for cognitive improvement? The implications of these questions pose ethical dilemmas confronting how we view meritocracy and achievement in the modern world.

Furthermore, the utilization of memory enhancements can lead to unintended consequences, where the intrinsic value of learning and collective knowledge may be overshadowed by an overemphasis on performance. If individuals rely heavily on external aids to enhance their memory, the essence of traditional learning—characterized by effort, exploration, and genuine understanding—could be compromised. This raises critical concerns about whether individuals, when equipped with cognitive enhancements, truly understand the material they are recalling or merely regurgitating information. The potential shift in focus from meaningful learning experiences to mere data retrieval invites reflections on the very nature of education and its long-held values.

In addition, the philosophical debate extends to the consequences of memory manipulation technologies. For instance, should individuals have the right to choose what memories to enhance, alter, or erase? The power to curate our memory significantly impacts our emotions and identity, elevating questions about consent, agency, and the ethical implications of such decisions. As we increasingly integrate cognitive enhancement technologies into our lives, the necessity of establishing clear ethical guidelines that govern memory manipulation becomes more pressing.

Moreover, discussions around the societal implications of cognitive enhancements often intersect with concerns surrounding the nature of intelligence and its measurement. A pivotal question arises: if individuals enhance their cognitive capabilities through technology, how do we redefine intelligence? Are we moving towards a conceptualization of intelligence that includes not only traditional markers —such as IQ tests or academic achievements—but also emotional intelligence, adaptability, and resilience? Addressing these broader dimensions can challenge conventional beliefs and inspire conversations that envision a more inclusive understanding of intelligence.

Another significant aspect of intellectual fairness involves the role of education in shaping cognitive enhancement practices. For educational systems to effectively address disparities, it is paramount to develop inclusive curricula that prioritize accessibility, adaptability, and the ethical implications of memory interventions. Educators must grapple with the responsibility of ensuring that students from all backgrounds can access cognitive tools, encouraging an equitable landscape where learners can thrive without the barriers posed by socioeconomic status.

In summary, the philosophical debates on intellectual fair play surrounding cognitive enhancements invite us to critically explore the nuances of equity, access, and the ethical dimensions of memory augmentation. As we navigate the complexities of enhancing memory and cognition in the contemporary world, it becomes increasingly vital to engage in open dialogues that encompass diverse perspectives. By recognizing the power dynamics associated with cognitive interventions and advocating for inclusive practices, we can work towards an equitable framework that honors individual agency and promotes fair intellectual pursuits for all. Ultimately, these discussions can guide us toward a future where cognitive enhancements enrich the learning experience while fostering a society rooted in ethical principles, empathy, and shared knowledge.

13.5. Cultural and Societal Reflections

As societies move forward in embracing cognitive enhancement techniques, the cultural and societal reflections on these advancements reveal a complex interplay of opportunities and challenges. Memory augmentation begs the question of its broader societal implications, not only on an individual level but also on a community scale. Cognitive enhancements, particularly those tied to memory techniques and innovations, have the potential to transform educational attainment, professional competencies, and personal growth. However, these advancements also require careful consideration of the ethical, social, and cultural dimensions.

In many cultures, the importance of memory and retaining knowledge has long been rooted in traditions and communal practices. Oral histories, storytelling, and communal memory techniques have historically played vital roles in sustaining cultural identity and preserving communal knowledge. As we explore contemporary memory augmentation techniques, we find ourselves at a critical junction where the age-old importance of memory converges with modern innovations. Memory techniques such as memory palaces, supplemented by technological advancements, signal a profound shift in how individuals interact with and view knowledge retention.

The efficacy of cognitive enhancements can also lead to concerns about the societal implications of unequal access to such technologies. As cognitive enhancement resources and digital memory tools become more prevalent, the potential for a divide between those with access and those without becomes apparent. Wealth disparities may translate into differences in educational access, leading to unequal opportunities for cognitive growth. Societies must engage in proactive efforts to democratize access to memory-enhancing technologies, ensuring that all individuals—regardless of socioeconomic status— can benefit from advancements in cognitive training.

In the workplace, the impact of memory augmentation techniques is equally notable. Professionals equipped with enhanced memory skills are better positioned to navigate complex tasks, recall vital information in client interactions, and thrive in dynamic and competitive environments. As such, organizations and institutions that embrace memory-enhancing techniques have the potential to create more efficient and innovative cultures. However, the prospect of cognitive enhancement in professional settings raises ethical questions about fair competition and the intrinsic value of learned knowledge.

Moreover, as cognitive interventions become increasingly mainstream, cultural perceptions of intelligence and memory may shift. The very definition of what it means to be intelligent might evolve to encompass not just raw cognitive ability but emotional intelligence, adaptability, and collaborative skills. Memory augmentations, then, can foster a new understanding of intelligence that celebrates a holistic approach, promoting strategies that empower individuals to thrive in diverse environments.

Popular culture plays a significant role in shaping societal narratives around memory enhancement, often highlighting both the promise and perils of cognitive augmentation. Literature, films, and television series frequently explore the transformative power of memory manipulation while delving into ethical dilemmas concerning individual agency. These cultural narratives provide rich terrain for discussions about the implications of cognitive enhancements, urging society to reflect on what enhancements mean for personal identity, agency, and community dynamics.

Culturally, disparities in how memory and cognitive skills are regarded can impact learning practices and retention techniques. In some societies, rote memorization may be undervalued in favor of interactive learning methods, while others might emphasize the importance of memorization in traditions. Understanding these cultural variations is crucial for designing effective and culturally sensitive memory enhancement strategies that resonate across diverse populations.

Furthermore, as cognitive enhancement technologies become more integrated into educational systems, the intersection of cultural values and memory techniques will shape the future of learning. Traditional views of education may shift from a focus on standardization to personalized learning paths that incorporate memory skills as foundational components. Education systems embracing cognitive diversity will recognize individual learners' unique memory techniques, valuing them as integral to their educational journeys.

In conclusion, the cultural and societal reflections on memory enhancement underscore its multifaceted implications on both individual and collective fronts. While cognitive enhancements hold immense promise for improving learning outcomes and fostering personal growth, the challenges of access, ethical considerations, and cultural perceptions remind us of the need for a balanced approach. Embracing memory-enhancing techniques with an appreciation for diversity, inclusivity, and ethical practices will ensure that society can harness the full potential of cognitive innovations while nurturing the essence of human experience. By honoring the cultural significance of memory, we can collectively build a future that not only values cognitive enhancement but also embodies the richness of human connection and understanding.

14. Health Perspectives on Memory Enhancement

14.1. Influence of Diet and Exercise

In the rapidly evolving landscape of human cognition, the influence of diet and exercise on memory and cognitive function is a crucial area of exploration. As we strive to understand and enhance our cognitive abilities, it becomes increasingly clear that lifestyle choices —particularly nutritional habits and physical activity—serve as foundational pillars for optimal brain health and resilience. This chapter delves deeply into how diet and exercise impact memory, ultimately highlighting the significant interplay between these lifestyle choices and cognitive functions.

The brain, like other organs in the body, requires proper nutrition to function optimally. Dietary choices have been shown to have profound effects on cognitive capabilities, including memory retention and recall. A well-balanced diet rich in essential nutrients is fundamental for neuroprotection and cognitive vitality. Specifically, certain nutrients play notable roles in supporting brain health:

1. Omega-3 Fatty Acids: These essential fats, found abundantly in fish, flaxseeds, and walnuts, are integral to maintaining neuronal integrity and promoting neurogenesis—the formation of new neurons. Research suggests that omega-3 fatty acids contribute to improved memory and cognitive processing, highlighting their anti-inflammatory properties and role in modulating neurotransmitters such as serotonin and dopamine.

2. Antioxidants: Nutrients such as vitamins C and E, found in fruits and vegetables, are critical in combating oxidative stress within the brain. Oxidative stress can impair cognitive function and lead to neurodegenerative diseases. Antioxidants help protect the brain by neutralizing free radicals, thereby fostering a healthier environment for memory encoding and retrieval.

3. Polyphenols: Found in colorful fruits, vegetables, tea, and dark chocolate, polyphenols have been shown to enhance memory and cognitive function. Studies indicate that polyphenols encourage neuroplasticity, supporting the brain's ability to form new connections and improve memory retention.

4. B Vitamins: Essential for energy metabolism and neurotransmitter synthesis, B vitamins (particularly B6, B12, and folate) have been linked to cognitive performance. Deficiencies in these vitamins can lead to cognitive decline and memory impairments. Adequate intake supports optimal brain function and enhances memory capacity.

The timing of meals also plays a significant role in cognitive function. Research has indicated that irregular eating patterns, particularly high sugar or processed food consumption, can lead to inflammation and cognitive impairments. Conversely, maintaining a stable eating schedule with balanced meals supports sustained energy levels conducive to cognitive processing.

In parallel with dietary habits, regular physical exercise has a profound impact on memory and overall cognitive function. Engaging in exercise boosts blood flow to the brain, enhancing oxygen and nutrient delivery. This has several positive effects on cognitive health:

1. Neurogenesis: Exercise fosters the production of brain-derived neurotrophic factor (BDNF), a protein crucial for supporting neurogenesis and synaptic plasticity. Increased levels of BDNF are associated with improved learning, memory retention, and higher levels of cognitive performance.

2. Stress Reduction: Physical activity helps lower cortisol levels, a hormone associated with stress. Chronic stress has detrimental effects on memory, particularly in the hippocampus, an area crucial for forming new memories. By promoting relaxation and enhancing mood, exercise creates an environment conducive to cognitive enhancement.

3. Cognitive Agility and Executive Function: Regular exercise, particularly aerobic activities, has been linked to improvements in cognitive agility, executive function, and information processing speed. These attributes are critical for effective problem-solving and decision-making, which often underline higher cognitive performance.

4. Social Engagement: Group activities or team sports create social interactions that provide cognitive stimulation, often simultaneously reducing anxiety and enhancing mood. The combined benefits of physical activity and social engagement bolster overall brain health and cognitive resilience.

Moreover, the benefits of diet and exercise on memory are not limited to direct cognitive enhancements; they also contribute to overall well-being, thereby reducing the likelihood of cognitive decline associated with aging. Initiatives promoting a healthy lifestyle can yield significant effects on brain health, manifesting in better memory performance and cognitive longevity.

In summary, the influence of diet and exercise on memory underscores the interconnection between physical well-being and cognitive function. A well-rounded diet rich in brain-boosting nutrients, coupled with regular physical activity, forms a holistic strategy for enhancing memory and cognitive performance. As we continue to explore the science behind memory, embracing lifestyle changes centered on proper nutrition and exercise will play a crucial role in fostering a healthier brain, ultimately empowering individuals to unlock their full cognitive potential. This crucial interplay between lifestyle choices and memory development paves the way for a future where cognitive enhancement through diet and exercise is not just a possibility but a vibrant reality for everyone.

14.2. Mental Health and Memory Techniques

In the realm of memory techniques, the relationship between mental health and cognitive enhancement is profound and multifaceted. Mental health significantly influences an individual's ability to process and retain information; therefore, understanding this interplay is essential for optimizing memory strategies and developing effective enhancement techniques. This chapter will explore the ways in which mental health affects memory capacity, the implications for treatment and training, and the necessity of integrating mental well-being into our cognitive enhancement initiatives.

The first key area to consider is the impact of mental health conditions, such as anxiety and depression, on memory function. Research indicates that these conditions are often correlated with memory impairments, particularly in working memory and episodic memory. For instance, anxiety can lead to difficulties in concentration, which disrupts the cognitive resources needed for encoding new information. When the mind is preoccupied with worry or distress, the capacity to focus on a task is diminished, impeding knowledge retention. Similarly, depression is linked to slower cognitive processing and challenges in recalling information, particularly when accessing emotionally charged memories. Understanding these dynamics highlights the critical importance of addressing mental health as a preliminary step in maximizing memory enhancement techniques.

Conversely, memory techniques can play an instrumental role in promoting mental health and overall well-being. Engaging with memory exercises, such as constructing memory palaces or employing mnemonic devices, provides individuals with structured activities that foster focus, creativity, and self-efficacy. Utilizing these techniques allows individuals to harness their cognitive skills in a way that can provide a sense of accomplishment, thereby combating feelings of inadequacy often associated with mental health challenges. Building a memory palace not only engages the mind therapeutically but can also serve as an emotional outlet, where individuals can explore ideas, assist in organizing their thoughts, and create rich narratives that reflect their experiences.

Moreover, the incorporation of mindfulness practices into memory techniques has shown promise in positively influencing mental health. Mindfulness—a state of active, open attention to the present

—enhances cognitive function by promoting relaxation and reducing stress. Integrating mindfulness with memory techniques can help individuals improve focus while practicing memory retrieval. For instance, engaging in mindful breathing exercises prior to utilizing a memory palace can ground individuals in the present moment, sharpening their concentration and ultimately leading to better recall. By fostering a connection between mental health and effective memory training, we create avenues for holistic cognitive improvement.

In exploring the therapeutic benefits of memory techniques, research has indicated that individuals with memory retrieval challenges—often linked to conditions such as PTSD or cognitive decline—can benefit from structured memory training programs. Interventions that emphasize the reconstruction of positive memories can empower individuals to challenge negative thought patterns, encouraging resilience and emotional healing. Therapeutic practices involving memory can guide individuals in reconfiguring their relationships with their own narrative, fostering a healthier emotional state while improving memory recall.

Additionally, the role of social connections in mental health cannot be overlooked when considering memory enhancement techniques. Sharing memory techniques in supportive group settings fosters collaboration and validation among participants. Engaging with peers promotes motivation, accountability, and emotional support—critical components that enhance both mental well-being and memory retention. In this way, memory training becomes a communal practice, bringing individuals together to learn, support one another, and collectively enhance cognitive skills.

As we move forward, integrating mental health considerations into cognitive enhancement initiatives is paramount. Educational institutions, workplaces, and mental health organizations should prioritize this integration, fostering awareness of the links between mental well-being and cognitive capabilities. Proactive mental health support through counseling or therapy can provide individuals with the necessary tools to balance stress, thereby enhancing their capacity to engage with memory techniques effectively.

In summary, the relationship between mental health and memory techniques is reciprocal and significant. Addressing mental health concerns is essential for optimizing cognitive enhancement while concurrently employing memory techniques to promote well-being and resilience. As we navigate the complexities of human cognition, it is vital to recognize that our mental states deeply influence our ability to learn and remember. By bridging memory enhancement strategies with mental health initiatives, we can create comprehensive approaches that empower individuals to thrive both cognitively and emotionally, enhancing their overall quality of life. As we shape memory training practices, it is crucial to embrace the interplay between mental health and memory, forging pathways that lead to enriched learning experiences and holistic well-being.

14.3. Supplements and Natural Enhancement

In this era of rapid technological advancement and increasing reliance on digital tools, the exploration of supplements and natural enhancement techniques for memory and cognitive function takes on paramount importance. The ability to bolster cognitive capacities through dietary choices, natural supplements, and holistic approaches offers individuals a proactive path to enhance their memory, thereby fostering personal growth, academic success, and professional excellence. This inquiry delves into the use of dietary strategies, naturally derived supplements, and lifestyle choices that synergistically promote memory enhancement.

At the forefront of natural enhancement approaches is the understanding that a well-nourished brain is critical for optimal cognitive performance. Nutritional science emphasizes that the key nutrients consumed directly influence brain health, functioning, and memory retention. Attention to diet must encompass a variety of foods rich in essential vitamins, minerals, antioxidants, and healthy fats—all of which provide the building blocks for robust cognitive function.

1. Healthy Fats: Omega-3 fatty acids, found in foods like fatty fish (salmon, mackerel), nuts, and seeds, have been shown to play a vital role in maintaining neuronal health and promoting neurogenesis. Consuming these healthy fats can improve synaptic plasticity, thus enhancing memory and learning capabilities.

2. Antioxidants: Berries—particularly blueberries—are rich in antioxidants, which combat oxidative stress and inflammation within the brain. Research has suggested that regular consumption of antioxidant-rich foods supports cognitive resilience and memory retention, thus making them powerful allies in the quest for cognitive enhancement.

3. Vitamins and Minerals: Certain B vitamins, particularly B6, B12, and folate, have been associated with improved cognitive function and reduced memory decline. Foods such as leafy greens, legumes, and fortified cereals can supply these essential nutrients, promoting optimal brain health.

4. Herbal Supplements: Natural supplements like ginkgo biloba and bacopa monnieri have garnered interest for their potential cognitive-enhancing effects. Research indicates that these herbs may improve memory performance through mechanisms that enhance blood flow to the brain and promote neuroprotective pathways.

5. Adaptogens: Herbs such as ashwagandha and rhodiola rosea are classified as adaptogens, which may help the body resist stress and promote cognitive clarity. Some studies suggest that these adaptogens can reduce anxiety and enhance the capacity to focus and retain information—vital components in memory enhancement.

In addition to dietary considerations, the integration of lifestyle choices—including exercise and mindfulness practices—plays a vital role in natural memory enhancement. Regular physical activity is instrumental in bolstering brain health by increasing blood flow, enhancing neuroplasticity, and stimulating the release of neurotransmitters associated with learning and memory. Engaging in aerobic exercises, resistance training, and even mindfulness practices such as yoga or meditation can improve mood, focus, and overall cognitive function.

Moreover, sleep quality emerges as a crucial factor influencing memory retention and cognitive performance. Consolidation of memories primarily occurs during sleep, making adequate restorative sleep essential for optimal cognitive function. Developing good sleep hygiene, including consistent sleep schedules and minimizing disruptions, fosters better memory processing and enhances learning outcomes.

Social engagement and emotional well-being further contribute to cognitive health. Building and maintaining strong social connections provide emotional support, reducing stress and enhancing overall mental health—both essential components of memory retention. In exploring natural enhancements for memory, it is paramount to recognize the holistic interplay between physical, social, emotional, and cognitive well-being.

As we consider the potential for natural enhancements to support memory capacity, it remains essential to approach these techniques with an evidence-based perspective. Individuals interested in using supplements or dietary changes to improve memory should consult reputable research and healthcare professionals to ensure that their approaches are safe and beneficial.

In conclusion, supplements and natural enhancement techniques offer promising avenues to support memory capacity and cognitive function. By focusing on dietary choices rich in essential nutrients, integrating exercise into daily routines, prioritizing sleep quality, and fostering social connections, individuals can adopt a proactive stance toward enhancing their cognitive well-being. Embracing these holistic approaches to memory enhancement is fundamental for fostering a healthier, more engaged mind—a pursuit that has the potential to enrich lives both academically and personally. As we navigate an increasingly information-rich world, embracing these natural enhancements empowers us to optimize our cognitive capabilities and thrive in our endeavors.

14.4. Preventing Cognitive Decline

Preventing cognitive decline is becoming increasingly vital as our understanding of aging and brain health evolves. The brain, like other organs, is susceptible to wear and deterioration over time. However, emerging research indicates that proactive measures can be taken to reduce the risk of cognitive decline and promote long-term brain health. This section explores various methods, strategies, and lifestyle choices that serve as preventive measures, promoting cognitive vitality throughout the lifespan.

The first pillar of cognitive health is a holistic approach that integrates physical health, mental stimulation, social engagement, and emotional well-being. One of the most significant lifestyle factors influencing cognitive health is regular physical exercise. Research has shown that aerobic exercise, in particular, increases blood flow to the brain, promotes neurogenesis (the birth of new neurons), and enhances synaptic plasticity. Engaging in regular physical activity stimulates the production of brain-derived neurotrophic factor (BDNF), a protein that is crucial for overall brain health. Incorporating activities like walking, swimming, or dancing can provide immediate benefits for cognitive function, reducing the risk of dementia-related diseases.

In addition to exercise, nutrition plays a central role in brain health. A balanced diet rich in essential nutrients supports cognitive function and can help prevent cognitive decline. Diets that emphasize the consumption of a variety of fruits, vegetables, whole grains, lean proteins, and healthy fats—which includes omega-3 fatty acids —have been associated with lower rates of cognitive impairment. The Mediterranean diet, for example, has gained recognition for its neuroprotective properties. An emphasis on antioxidants, vitamins, minerals, and healthy fats not only sustains overall health but also offers long-term protection against cognitive decline.

Mental stimulation is another critical component of cognitive health and should not be overlooked. Engaging in intellectually stimulating activities—such as reading, playing musical instruments, solving puzzles, or participating in brain-training exercises—can help build cognitive reserves. Neuroplasticity—the brain's ability to adapt and reorganize itself—suggests that lifelong learning and mental challenges are crucial for maintaining brain function as we age. Memory techniques, including memory palaces, play a pivotal part in this stimulation by encouraging individuals to exercise their cognitive abilities actively.

Social engagement is equally essential for cognitive health. The emotional and cognitive benefits of maintaining social connections have been well-documented; having a robust social network can mitigate feelings of isolation and depression, both of which are risk factors for cognitive decline. Participating in community activities, attending social events, or even engaging in virtual conversations with friends and family can provide crucial social engagement that supports both mental and emotional well-being.

Moreover, emotional health is intrinsically linked to cognitive function. Chronic stress, anxiety, and depression can adversely affect memory and cognitive capabilities. Mindfulness practices, such as meditation and yoga, cultivate emotional regulation and stress management, promoting relaxation and mental clarity. Techniques that encourage emotional awareness facilitate positive mental states that enhance cognitive performance and resilience against cognitive decline.

As we further examine prevention strategies, it is important to acknowledge the role of preventive health care measures in facilitating cognitive health. Routine health check-ups, monitoring potential risk factors such as hypertension, diabetes, and hyperlipidemia, and adhering to prescribed medical interventions can significantly impact cognitive outcomes over time. Individuals should remain proactive in seeking guidance from healthcare professionals regarding cognitive health, exploring personalized strategies that best suit their circumstances.

Finally, an increased awareness of the evidential nature of cognitive decline among healthcare communities and the broader society is essential. Advocacy for cognitive health education, both among healthcare providers and the general public, can raise awareness about risk factors and available preventative measures. Establishing programs aimed at promoting brain health, coupled with supportive policies for mental health initiatives, can produce a culture that values cognitive health across the lifespan.

In conclusion, preventing cognitive decline is not solely a response to aging, but an ongoing endeavor that reflects a commitment to holistic living. By integrating regular exercise, balanced nutrition, mental stimulation, social engagement, emotional health, and proactive health care measures, individuals can take actionable steps toward sustaining cognitive vitality. As we embrace these strategies, we pave the way for a future where cognitive health remains a priority, allowing us to enjoy richer, more fulfilling lives as we age. Emphasizing prevention and sustaining brain health ultimately reflect a broader view of well-being that recognizes the profound interplay between body, mind, and social connection.

14.5. Integration of Wellness with Memory Training

The integration of wellness with memory training represents a vital intersection of cognitive enhancement and holistic health. Understanding that memory and overall well-being are interdependent allows us to craft strategies not only for improved retention but also for enriching the human experience. As research continues to reveal the complex interplay between mental, physical, and emotional health, we can begin to explore how practices that nurture wellness can be seamlessly woven into memory training techniques—leading to significant improvements in cognitive function and memory performance.

At the heart of this integration lies the recognition that our mental state profoundly influences our memory capabilities. Stress, anxiety, and other negative emotional states can create barriers to effective learning and recall. When our minds are clouded by emotional turmoil, the cognitive processes essential for memory encoding and retrieval can be impaired. For instance, high levels of cortisol—a hormone released during stress—can hinder the functioning of the hippocampus, a brain region crucial for forming new memories. Therefore, addressing emotional wellness becomes not only a matter of fostering overall well-being but also a foundational component of cognitive enhancement.

Incorporating mindfulness practices into memory training can help counteract these negative effects. Mindfulness techniques, such as meditation and deep breathing, promote relaxation and emotional regulation, creating a mental environment conducive to memory retention. By teaching individuals to focus their attention and reduce cognitive overload, mindfulness practices enhance the encoding of information in ways that directly improve memory performance. Integrating these techniques into memory training courses or programs ensures that learners are equipped with the tools needed to succeed while also tending to their mental health.

Physical wellness also plays an essential role in memory enhancement. Regular exercise has been shown to have substantial benefits for cognitive function, promoting the production of neurotrophic factors that support brain health. Aerobic activities, particularly, stimulate the release of brain-derived neurotrophic factor (BDNF), which is associated with improved memory function and neurogenesis. Therefore, structuring memory training programs to include physical activity—whether it's integrating short exercise breaks during study sessions or promoting active learning that requires movement—can enhance cognitive performance while fostering physical health.

Nutrition is another vital aspect of pairing wellness with memory training. Specific nutrients—such as omega-3 fatty acids, antioxidants, and B vitamins—are critical for optimal brain function.

Developing educational resources that highlight the importance of a balanced diet rich in these nutrients can empower individuals to make dietary choices that support their cognitive health. Integrating these insights into memory training workshops or courses enables participants to cultivate both their memory skills and their overall wellness simultaneously, creating a holistic approach to cognitive enhancement.

Furthermore, social and emotional support can amplify the effects of memory training initiatives. Initiatives that promote collaboration and peer interaction foster environments where learners feel supported, connected, and emotionally secure. When individuals can share their experiences and insights related to memory techniques, they enrich the collective learning environment, making it more conducive to effective memory retention. Facilitating supportive communities—whether through workshops, online forums, or peer-focused study groups—creates a culture of wellness that enhances the overall impact of memory training.

As we anticipate future developments in memory training integration with wellness practices, it becomes increasingly clear that this holistic approach will result in a new paradigm for cognitive enhancement. Programs that recognize the interconnectedness of physical health, emotional well-being, and cognitive capacities will likely emerge as the standard. This paradigm shift invites educational institutions, workplaces, and healthcare professionals to prioritize comprehensive frameworks that address wellness in conjunction with memory skills training.

In summary, the integration of wellness with memory training serves as a cornerstone for enhancing cognitive performance. By addressing mental and physical health factors through mindfulness practices, physical activities, nutritional education, and social support, individuals can significantly boost their memory capabilities while nurturing their overall well-being. As we explore this synergistic approach, we forge pathways toward a future in which memory enhancement techniques embrace the holistic nature of human experience, championing the idea that memory is not only a cognitive function but a vital part of our collective journey toward personal growth, learning, and fulfillment.

15. Global Initiatives and Collaborative Innovations

15.1. Global Perspectives on Memory Technology

As our understanding of memory technology and cognitive enhancement deepens, it becomes increasingly clear that these advancements have significant global implications. A comprehensive examination of global perspectives on memory technology reveals the diverse approaches and initiatives employed worldwide to enhance human cognition and memory retention. From groundbreaking research to innovative applications of memory techniques, these efforts showcase a commitment to improving cognitive abilities on a global scale.

Countries across the globe are investing in cognitive enhancement technologies that forge new pathways for memory retention and utilization. In the United States, initiatives focusing on brain health have surged, particularly in the realm of digital memory aids. Leading tech companies are developing applications that integrate memory training techniques with artificial intelligence, offering personalized learning experiences that help users optimize their memory performance. This evolution emphasizes the need for collaboration between cognitive scientists, technologists, and educational institutions to ensure that the advancements benefit all users.

In Europe, several countries prioritize research into memory enhancement through public funding and institutional support. Collaborative projects are emerging in areas such as neuroscience, psychology, and cognitive science, uniting researchers from different nations to explore innovative memory techniques. For instance, the European Commission has funded initiatives aimed at utilizing neuroplasticity principles to develop memory training programs that can be widely implemented in educational and professional sectors. These collaborative efforts reflect a commitment to fostering a shared understanding of cognitive enhancement, as nations leverage their collective expertise to address common challenges.

Different perspectives on memory technology can also be observed in Asia, where nations like Japan and South Korea are leading the way in adopting cognitive enhancement tools within educational frameworks. In these countries, there is a strong emphasis on integrating technology into classroom environments, where memory techniques are regularly practiced using digital tools. Japanese schools, for example, have introduced digital platforms that employ spaced repetition and gamified learning to improve student retention rates, encouraging a culture of memory enhancement that aligns with modern educational practices.

Global perspectives extend to Africa, where there is a growing recognition of the importance of memory enhancement for educational access and equity. Initiatives aimed at distributing cognitive tools and memory training resources are gaining traction, addressing the unique challenges posed by limited access to quality education in many regions. Collaborative efforts between governments, nongovernmental organizations, and educational institutions are focused on providing resources and support to underserved communities, emphasizing the need for inclusive access to cognitive enhancement techniques.

In addition to these specific regional efforts, collaborative research initiatives are emerging as a vital facet of advancing memory technology on a global scale. Scholars from diverse fields—ranging from cognitive neuroscience and psychology to education and technology —are forming partnerships that transcend borders. This global collaboration fosters innovation by encapsulating a breadth of expertise and perspectives, ultimately leading to advancements in our understanding of memory processes and techniques.

Furthermore, the role of policy in encouraging innovation in the field of cognitive enhancement cannot be overlooked. Policymakers have the ability to shape the direction of research and development by providing funding, establishing ethical guidelines, and creating supportive environments for cognitive technology initiatives. Governments can incentivize research partnerships between academic institutions and private industries, facilitating the development of memory technologies that are grounded in solid scientific principles.

Promoting accessibility to cognitive tools on a global scale is also paramount in harnessing the full potential of memory technology. Various initiatives are underway to ensure that cognitive enhancement resources—such as mobile applications and digital platforms—are translated into multiple languages and made available to diverse populations. Efforts to bridge the digital divide, particularly in underprivileged regions, are crucial in promoting equity in educational access and cognitive skill development.

Looking to the future, the potential for international collaboration in cognitive efforts appears promising. Collaborative platforms that facilitate knowledge sharing, joint research projects, and global forums for discussing advancements in memory techniques may become increasingly prevalent. These efforts can integrate local cultural contexts into cognitive enhancement practices, ensuring that innovative memory strategies resonate with diverse populations.

In conclusion, global perspectives on memory technology reveal a rich tapestry of initiatives and collaborations aimed at enhancing human cognition. Countries worldwide are approaching cognitive enhancement through a variety of lenses, fostering innovative research, educational practices, and policy frameworks that prioritize memory retention and cognitive development. As we explore and embrace the possibilities of memory technology on a global scale, we can pave the way for a future where cognitive enhancement is inclusive, effective, and grounded in a shared commitment to improving the human experience. By leveraging these diverse perspectives, we stand poised to advance memory technology and cognitive enhancement, ultimately enriching lives around the world.

15.2. Collaborative Research Initiatives

In the context of collaborative research initiatives, the landscape of memory enhancement is rich with multidisciplinary partnerships that seek to advance our understanding of cognition while addressing practical applications. These initiatives underscore the importance of collaboration among researchers across various fields, such as cognitive science, neuroscience, psychology, and technology, to explore innovative methodologies for enhancing memory and coping with the complexities of human cognition.

Over the past few decades, collaborative research efforts have facilitated synergies that transcend traditional academic boundaries. One prominent example comes from the intersection of cognitive neuroscience and educational psychology, where researchers actively examine how brain functions, such as neuroplasticity, influence memory retention. By gathering insights from both domains, interdisciplinary teams work together to design educational programs and memory training techniques that are empirically validated, ultimately aiming to support learners of all ages in optimizing their memory potential.

Moreover, international collaborations are increasingly common as scholars recognize the global challenges associated with cognitive enhancement. Sharing resources and expertise across countries enables researchers to explore diverse perspectives on memory techniques and their applications in various contexts. For example, projects focusing on the adverse effects of cognitive decline in aging populations have led to collaborative research initiatives that bridge studies from Europe, North America, and Australia. By pooling data and resources, researchers can identify commonalities and differences in cognitive aging patterns, fostering strategies for memory enhancement that are both culturally relevant and scientifically sound.

Public and private partnerships also play a critical role in advancing research initiatives related to memory enhancement. By forming alliances with industry stakeholders, academic researchers can access funding, technological tools, and practical insights into implementing memory techniques at scale. These partnerships often lead to the development of innovative cognitive training platforms that incorporate evidence-based memory strategies, providing individuals with accessible tools for improving their cognitive abilities. Such initiatives demonstrate how collaboration between academia and industry can drive real-world applications, ensuring that rigorous research influences practical cognitive enhancement methods.

Additionally, the role of government-sponsored research grants and initiatives cannot be overlooked. Many countries have recognized the importance of cognitive health and memory in advancing education and quality of life. This recognition has led to increased investment in scientific research focused on understanding memory processes and developing novel enhancement techniques. Collaborative efforts among universities, research institutions, and government agencies enable the exploration of pressing cognitive challenges while establishing research priorities that reflect societal needs.

In the context of educational reform, collaborative research initiatives become vital for reshaping curricula to incorporate memory enhancement techniques effectively. Schools and universities that embrace a collective approach to memory research can design evidence-based educational frameworks that prioritize memory development from early learning to higher education. Integrating insights from diverse fields ensures that cognitive strategies resonate with learners holistically, fostering environments where memory techniques become integral to the learning process.

Finally, global forums and symposia serve as venues for scholars, researchers, educators, and policy makers to come together and share advancements in memory research. These collaborative discussions help forge international bonds and inspire further innovation while keeping the focus on ethical standards, inclusive practices, and the interconnectedness of knowledge sharing across borders.

In summary, collaborative research initiatives play a pivotal role in advancing our understanding of memory enhancement and cognitive processes. By bridging gaps across disciplines, inviting international partnerships, fostering public and private collaborations, and encouraging educational reform grounded in empirical evidence, the collective efforts of scholars and researchers pave the way for innovative ways to improve memory retention and cognitive performance. These initiatives not only deepen our understanding of cognition but also ensure that memory enhancement strategies reach diverse populations, enriching the global pursuit of knowledge and cognitive growth.

15.3. The Role of Policy in Encouraging Innovation

In a world where the mantra of "innovation drives progress" increasingly holds value, the role of policy in fostering an environment where creativity and progress flourish cannot be underestimated. Policy shapes the infrastructure of research and enables innovation through financial support, collaborative networks, and regulations that encourage or hinder experimentation. In the realm of cognitive enhancement and memory improvement, thoughtful and strategically implemented policies can unlock unprecedented advancements in technology, methodology, and societal applications.

At the heart of effective policy is the recognition of cognitive enhancement as a field with immense potential to benefit individuals and society at large. Policymakers must consider the implications of cognitive science on education, health care, and workforce development, realizing that investing in these areas yields exponential returns by enhancing cognitive capabilities and efficiency across many sectors. By prioritizing research funding for cognitive enhancement projects, policymakers can create a fertile ground for innovation where researchers, educators, and technologists work together to develop effective memory techniques and cognitive tools.

Furthermore, establishing frameworks for collaboration across academia, industry, and government can lead to breakthroughs in cognitive research. Policies that encourage the sharing of data, resources, and expertise can foster multidisciplinary approaches that yield more effective cognitive training techniques. Collaborative platforms, centers of innovation, and consortia focused on cognitive enhancement can emerge as vital players in this endeavor, streamlining research efforts while creating an environment that prioritizes shared knowledge and progress.

Alternatively, policymakers must also consider the ethical implications of cognitive enhancements, particularly in areas such as data privacy, informed consent, and equitable access. As digital memory techniques and cognitive tools evolve, the safeguarding of individual privacy rights is paramount. Ensuring that users are fully informed about how their personal cognitive data is collected and used fosters trust and accountability. An ethical framework that governs the use of cognitive technologies will not only protect individuals but also create a conducive atmosphere for innovation.

In addition to ethical considerations, policymakers must advocate for equitable access to cognitive enhancement tools and techniques, ensuring that all individuals have the opportunity to benefit from advancements. By distributing resources fairly and creating programs targeting underprivileged communities, policymakers can help bridge the cognitive gap that often arises from disparities in access to quality education and cognitive training. Technology should serve as an equalizer in cognitive development, helping individuals from diverse backgrounds improve their memory and cognitive capabilities.

Moreover, the importance of interdisciplinary collaboration in policy formulation cannot be overstated. Memory enhancement and cognitive technology spans a variety of fields, including neuroscience, psychology, education, computer science, and ethics. Engaging experts from these domains when developing cognitive enhancement policies allows for a well-rounded perspective that considers diverse viewpoints. Such collaboration can lead to policies grounded in solid evidence and driven by the latest advancements in research.

The global nature of cognitive enhancement initiatives also calls for international policies that foster collaboration across borders. Understanding that cognitive enhancement is a shared challenge and opportunity for humanity encourages partnerships among nations, leading to cross-cultural exchanges of ideas, techniques, and insights. Policies can facilitate research collaborations and knowledge sharing, creating a collective effort toward advancing memory technologies and cognitive enhancement techniques on a global stage.

The future of cognitive enhancement policy may also encompass a dynamic feedback mechanism, wherein the impacts of initiatives are actively monitored and evaluated. This adaptive approach allows policymakers to refine strategies and optimize investments in cognitive research and education continuously. Stakeholder engagement—through community forums, feedback surveys, and interdisciplinary panels—will enhance transparency and responsiveness within policy frameworks.

In conclusion, the role of policy in encouraging innovation within the realm of cognitive enhancement is both significant and multifaceted. By investing in research, fostering collaboration, emphasizing ethical considerations, ensuring equitable access, and engaging interdisciplinary approaches, policymakers can create the conditions necessary for innovation to thrive. Cognitive enhancement and memory improvement are poised to redefine notions of intelligence and learning, and thoughtful policy measures will be vital in harnessing the potential of these advancements for the betterment of society as a whole. As we continue to explore the boundaries of cognitive enhancement, a commitment to supportive policy frameworks will pave the way for transformative pathways that enhance memory, learning, and human potential.

15.4. Improving Accessibility Worldwide

In the pursuit of enhanced cognitive capabilities, the importance of improving accessibility to memory enhancement resources on a global scale cannot be overstated. As cognitive tools become more developed and increasingly integrated into our lives, efforts must be made to ensure that these advancements benefit individuals from all backgrounds, particularly those in underprivileged or underserved communities. Improved accessibility to memory enhancement techniques can serve as a catalyst for positive change, fostering equity in knowledge acquisition and cognitive development across varied demographics.

One pivotal element in enhancing accessibility worldwide is the democratization of technology. Digital memory tools, such as mobile apps and educational platforms, represent an invaluable resource for improving memory retention and cognitive function. Initiatives aimed at providing free or low-cost access to these tools can empower learners and individuals seeking to optimize their memory skills. Community workshops, online tutorials, and collaborative partnerships with educational institutions can facilitate the dissemination of knowledge about cognitive techniques, reaching populations that may lack access to conventional educational resources. By cultivating an ecosystem where cognitive tools are widely available, we can foster diverse learning environments that stimulate memory development regardless of socioeconomic status.

Moreover, addressing language barriers is crucial in expanding global accessibility to memory enhancement resources. The development of multilingual platforms and tools ensures that cognitive techniques are comprehensible and applicable to a wider audience. This entails not only translating existing content but also adapting memory techniques to culturally relevant contexts. Localizing memory strategies to resonate with specific cultural frameworks fosters greater engagement and understanding among diverse populations. Such customized approaches can significantly influence learning outcomes, allowing individuals worldwide to harness the power of memory enhancing techniques.

Incorporating community-driven projects further supports the improvement of accessibility by tailoring cognitive tools and resources to regional needs. Collaborative initiatives that include local educators, mental health professionals, and community leaders can provide deeper insights into the specific challenges faced by populations in their respective contexts. By empowering communities to take charge of their learning experiences, we create a sustainable framework for memory enhancement that resonates with the lived realities of those involved. For instance, programs focused on integrating memory techniques within cultural practices—such as oral storytelling traditions—can greatly stimulate cognitive engagement while preserving community heritage.

Additionally, investing in research aimed at understanding the unique cognitive challenges faced by marginalized communities can guide the development of targeted memory enhancements. Communities may experience varying degrees of cognitive stressors attributed to socioeconomic disparities or educational inequities, which can impact memory and learning capabilities. By conducting research that explores these challenges, policymakers and educators can design interventions tailored to specific group needs, ultimately optimizing memory development practices.

Education systems play a pivotal role in fostering accessibility to memory enhancement techniques. Curriculum reforms that prioritize the integration of cognitive tools—which include memory techniques as foundational elements of learning—create environments where all students can thrive. By embedding memory strategies in early childhood education, educators can establish strong cognitive foundations that extend throughout learners' academic journeys. Collaborative efforts between educational institutions and community organizations can enhance outreach initiatives aimed at sharing memory techniques with parents, caregivers, and community members, thus enriching the learning ecosystem.

Furthermore, the continuous exploration of ethical implications surrounding cognitive enhancements must remain central to advancing accessibility. As cognitive tools become more prevalent, discussions surrounding data privacy and informed consent will be paramount. Ensuring that users understand their rights and the implications of using cognitive technologies fosters an environment of trust and transparency. Accessible resources that emphasize ethical principles in cognitive enhancement can help promote responsible usage while nurturing informed communities.

In conclusion, improving accessibility to memory enhancement resources worldwide represents a vital objective in the quest for equitable educational opportunities and cognitive development. By democratizing technology, addressing language barriers, supporting community-driven initiatives, conducting research tailored to the unique challenges of marginalized populations, and incorporating cognitive tools into educational systems, we can lay the groundwork for a future where the benefits of cognitive enhancement techniques are accessible to all. As we navigate the complexities of memory enhancement, a collective commitment to fostering equity and inclusivity will ultimately shape a more knowledgeable and connected society, where everyone can unlock the potential of their cognitive capabilities.

Looking beyond accessibility, we must also contemplate the future of international cognitive efforts. Collaborative steps in the domain of cognitive enhancement hold the potential to transcend borders and foster a global environment of innovation and shared learning. As we face the challenges of an increasingly interconnected world, international cognitive initiatives provide a framework for knowledge exchange, resource sharing, and collective advancement in memory techniques.

International collaborations can take many forms, ranging from joint research programs that explore cognitive enhancement methodologies in diverse cultural contexts to cross-border partnerships that facilitate the distribution of memory enhancement tools. By pooling resources and leveraging the strengths of various academic institutions, governments, and organizations, we can create a rich tapestry of cognitive enhancement practices that resonate across cultural boundaries.

Furthermore, the integration of digital platforms enables unprecedented opportunities for global learners to engage with one another. Online courses and forums provide spaces for sharing and discussing cognitive techniques, fostering an atmosphere of open exchange that transcends geographical constraints. Such interconnectedness not only enriches the learning experience but also encourages the development of memory techniques that are culturally relevant and widely applicable.

In addition, international cognitive efforts can emphasize the importance of ethical considerations and responsible cognitive enhancement methodologies. Establishing global standards for cognitive enhancement practices ensures that all participants adhere to protocols that prioritize the agency and well-being of individuals. By fostering conversations on ethical frameworks and sharing insights from diverse cultural perspectives, we can cultivate a global discourse that champions the responsible use of memory techniques and cognitive interventions.

Ultimately, the future of international cognitive efforts holds the promise of collective progress and innovation. By embracing the diversity of human experience and fostering collaborations that ignite creativity, researchers and practitioners can pioneer new avenues for memory enhancement while addressing the unique challenges faced by individuals in various contexts. As we embark on this journey—one defined by shared learning, cultural richness, and ethical considerations—we empower future generations to navigate the complexities of cognition and memory, equipping them with the tools they need to thrive in an ever-evolving world.

In summary, the future of international cognitive efforts invites a transformative landscape for memory enhancement, driven by collaboration, inclusivity, and innovation. By tapping into global perspectives, knowledge, and resources, we can collectively champion the advancements in memory techniques that promise to enrich our understanding of cognition. In doing so, we forge a path toward a more equitable, just, and knowledgeable world where memory enhancement serves as a bridge connecting diverse cultures and fostering a shared commitment to cognitive excellence.

- The Science of Remembering: An Evolutionary Perspective
  - Memory in Primitive Societies Content: Memory in primitive societies serves as a critical foundation for understanding how early humans encoded vital survival information. In ancient communities, memory played an indispensable role in navigating complex environments, preserving cultural knowledge, and fostering so-

cial cohesion. This exploration emphasizes the significance of memory within primitive societies, uncovering the techniques and strategies that defined early memory practices and shaped the evolution of human cognition.

In primitive societies, memory systems were directly linked to survival, as individuals relied on their ability to recall essential information related to hunting, gathering, navigating their territories, and social interactions. Oral traditions emerged as the primary means of preserving knowledge and experiences within these communities. Storytelling served as a powerful mnemonic tool that enabled individuals to convey vital information to younger generations, ensuring that valuable skills, cultural practices, and environmental knowledge were transmitted effectively across time.

The use of vivid imagery and metaphor in oral traditions further facilitated memory encoding in primitive societies. Stories often contained rich sensory experiences that engaged the imagination and evoked emotions, ensuring that the information would be more easily remembered. For instance, hunters recounted tales of successful hunts, weaving in details about specific locations, animal behaviors, and seasonal changes. By attaching knowledge to narratives filled with vivid imagery, early humans developed a robust framework for recalling critical information essential for their health and survival.

Additionally, memory strategies in primitive cultures were often constructed around communal experiences and collaborative learning. Cognitive engagement flourished in social contexts, where individuals would practice memory techniques together. Group storytelling sessions, rituals, and shared activities created a supportive learning environment where community members reinforced each other's memories, deepening knowledge retention and cultural identity. This participatory approach to memory not only facilitated education but also strengthened interpersonal bonds, fostering cohesion in tribal or social settings.

The encoding of memory in primitive societies also intersected with the natural environment. Certain landscapes, landmarks, or seasonal changes were often imbued with cultural significance, acting as physical cues that anchored memories in terrain. By connecting memory to the landscape, individuals developed spatial awareness that aided navigation and resource management—a vital aspect of survival. The use of these environmental cues parallels modern memory techniques like the Method of Loci, emphasizing the age-old connection between memory, space, and human experience.

Memory was considered an adaptive trait in early human evolution, contributing to both cognitive development and social organization. The ability to recall information related to social dynamics, alliances, and resource availability directly impacted survival rates and community sustainability. As humans adapted to their surroundings and evolved socially, the depth and complexity of memory function also flourished, ultimately influencing the trajectory of human cognition.

In summary, memory in primitive societies reveals a fascinating interplay between survival, cultural transmission, and social cohesion. Oral traditions, vivid storytelling, communal learning, and environmental cues formed the backbone of memory practices, ensuring survival and cultural continuity. This exploration offers critical insights into how memory has played a central role throughout human evolution, highlighting the adaptive nature of memory in shaping our understanding of the world and ourselves.

Understanding memory in primitive societies not only enhances our appreciation for the resilience of human cognition but also illuminates pathways to cognitive enhancement in contemporary contexts. By embracing the techniques honed by our ancestors, we can draw upon the rich legacy of memory practices that continue to hold relevance in our quest for knowledge, creativity, and personal growth. As we step into the future, the foundational strategies from primitive cultures serve as a reminder of the enduring power of memory— the bridge that connects us to our past, our communities, and our potential for growth.

- Evolutionary Necessity: Why We Remember Content: The evolutionary necessity of memory highlights the crucial role that remembering plays in the survival and adaptation of species throughout history. Memory is not merely an academic concept; it embodies a practical and essential function that enables individuals to navigate the complexities of their environments, learn from experiences, and make informed decisions. This exploration delves into the evolutionary advantages that memory confers, underscoring its significance in shaping human cognition and behavior.

From an evolutionary perspective, the capacity to remember is integral to survival. Early humans relied on their memory to encode essential information related to food sources, predator behavior, environmental changes, and social dynamics within their groups. The ability to recall successful foraging routes, recognize potential threats, and identify kin and allies directly influenced an individual's chances of survival and reproductive success. Those with superior memory skills—capable of navigating their surroundings and retaining critical knowledge—were more likely to thrive and pass on their genetic material to subsequent generations.

As humans evolved, the complexity of their environments increased, necessitating more advanced memory capabilities. With the rise of social structures, the importance of remembering individuals, their relationships, and group dynamics became paramount. Social memory significantly impacted cooperation among early humans, fostering deeper emotional connections and alliances within communities. Remembering who to trust, who posed potential threats, and whom to cooperate with was essential for survival, leading to enhanced social cohesion and collaborative efforts.

Moreover, the evolution of memory serves as an underlying mechanism for learning and adaptation. As individuals encountered new experiences, memory facilitated the encoding of relevant information, ensuring that successful strategies were retained while mistakes were learned from and avoided in the future. This capacity for learning through experience provided early humans with an adaptive edge, allowing them to respond effectively to fluctuating circumstances in their environment.

The role of memory extends beyond individual survival to encompass collective knowledge within communities. Groups that harnessed shared memories through storytelling and oral traditions could transmit valuable knowledge—including survival strategies and cultural practices—from one generation to the next. This collective memory preserved essential wisdom and fostered resilience against challenges, ultimately enhancing the adaptive capacity of human societies.

Furthermore, the emotional dimensions of memory play a pivotal role in shaping behavior. Memories associated with emotional significance—whether positive or negative—tend to be recalled more vividly and readily, ensuring that individuals learn from emotionally charged experiences. Emotionally laden memories can inform decision-making, promoting self-preservation and the avoidance of harmful situations.

As we consider the evolutionary necessity of memory, it becomes evident that it is an invaluable asset that shapes our cognitive landscape. Today, this evolutionary legacy manifests in our ability to learn, adapt, and innovate in response to the ever-changing world. The vital lessons from our evolutionary history emphasize the importance of developing effective memory enhancement techniques—underscoring our connection to the past as we navigate the complexities of our present and future.

In summary, the necessity of memory from an evolutionary perspective reveals its critical role in survival, learning, and social cohesion. The capacity to encode and recall information has long been essential for adaptation, shaping the trajectory of human evolution. By understanding the foundations of why we remember—encompassing survival instincts, emotional insights, and collective knowledge—we gain profound insights into the mechanisms underpinning human cognition. As we delve into the realm of memory enhancement, these evolutionary principles invite us to embrace our capacity for growth and resilience, illuminating pathways toward a future that values memory as a cornerstone of human experience.

- Adaptive Memory Theory Content: Adaptive memory theory posits that the ability to remember is not merely a product of cognitive function; rather, it serves a crucial evolutionary purpose that enhances individuals' adaptability to their environments. This theoretical framework emphasizes that memory evolved to support actions that maximized survival and reproductive success, positioning it as a vital aspect of human evolution. By examining this theory, we can better understand the significance of memory and its adaptive nuances in contemporary contexts, ultimately guiding the development of effective enhancement techniques.

The kernel of adaptive memory theory lies in the proposition that our memory systems are attuned to specific types of information that bear relevance to survival. Research suggests that humans tend to remember information that is emotionally charged or contextual—such as the location of food sources or potential dangers—at higher rates than more neutral details. This phenomenon underscores the adaptive function of memory, allowing individuals to retain knowledge critical for navigating complex environments.

One prominent example of adaptive memory is the encoding of spatial navigational information. Throughout our evolutionary history, the ability to remember locations and routes significantly impacted foraging behaviors and resource management. The hippocampus, a brain region critical for spatial memory, evolved as an essential component for helping early humans navigate their terrains with efficacy. Studies have shown that the way we encode memories about places is intricately tied to our survival instincts; thus, the brain's architecture reflects this evolutionary imperative.

Moreover, the emotional salience of experiences heavily influences what we remember. Research reveals that emotionally charged events lead to stronger and more vivid memories. For example, individuals are more likely to remember personal milestones—such as a wedding or a graduation—because of the emotions associated with these experiences. Adaptive memory theory suggests that this mechanism is an evolutionary adaptation to prioritize the retention of information that informs our decision-making and social affiliations—the result being meaningful connections that enhance our chances of success in social environments.

Contemporary implications of adaptive memory theory extend beyond survival; they suggest that memory processes can be consciously refined to respond to modern informational needs. For example, in today's data-saturated environment, understanding how adaptive processes play into memory techniques can help individuals optimize their learning. By leveraging the principles of adaptive memory, one can create memory palaces that explicitly focus on emotionally salient or contextual knowledge. By enriching learning experiences with narratives infused with emotional relevance, learners can enhance retention and application.

In addition to individual applications, adaptive memory theory invites exploration into memory enhancement interventions within educational and professional settings. Programs designed to prioritize emotionally engaging and context-driven learning can profoundly impact outcomes. By integrating adaptive principles into curricula, educators can foster an environment that values meaningful engagement with the material, maximizing memory retention and enhancing cognitive flexibility.

As we consider the future trajectory of adaptive memory theory, the integration of neuroscience and technology continues to inspire innovative practices. Advances in neuroimaging and cognitive research can inform the development of cognitive training tools designed to work in tandem with our adaptive memory systems. However, as we advance, it is essential to engage in discussions surrounding ethical considerations—especially concerning the facilitation of cognitive enhancements that retain the core tenets of individual agency and inclusivity.

In summary, adaptive memory theory illustrates that memory serves an evolutionary purpose, aiding individuals in navigating complex environments and making informed decisions. This understanding bridges historical context with contemporary applications, guiding efforts to create effective memory enhancement techniques that resonate with modern learners. By embracing the nuances of adaptive memory, we deepen our appreciation for the intricacies of human cognition while fostering a resilient approach to the challenges posed by memory in our ever-evolving world.

- The Future of Evolution in Cognition Content: As we contemplate the future of evolution in cognition, it becomes increasingly clear that the interplay between memory, intelligence, and technological advancements may shape the trajectory of human development in unprecedented ways. Cognitive evolution will not only be influenced by our biological makeup but also by how we engage with and adapt to our changing environments—foreseen and unforeseen —including the proliferation of cognitive enhancement technologies, digital memory tools, and evolving educational paradigms.

One promising area for future cognitive evolution lies in the continued journey of neuroplasticity: the brain's capacity to adapt and rewire itself based on experience. As we actively engage in memory training techniques and cognitive exercises, we stimulate neuroplastic changes that enhance our cognitive capabilities. The more we practice memory techniques—like mental imagery, storytelling, or the Method of Loci—the more our neural networks strengthen. This suggests that our ability to adapt cognitively may become increasingly pronounced with dedicated practice, indicating a future where mastering memory techniques shapes cognitive prowess.

The integration of technology in education, work, and personal growth serves as a critical driver steering evolution in cognition. The pocket-sized computing power we carry in smartphones complements our cognitive capabilities, enabling new ways of learning and retaining information. However, the relationship between technology and cognitive evolution presents both opportunities and challenges;

while technology enhances memory capacity, there exists a risk of dependency on these tools, as individuals may forgo developing intrinsic memory skills in favor of convenience. Society must thus navigate these complexities carefully—striving to balance technological augmentation with a commitment to fostering enduring cognitive skills and nurture a growth mindset.

Moreover, the global exchange of knowledge and ideas in an interconnected digital landscape sets the stage for cognitive evolution on a collective scale. The availability of information and online learning resources encourages diverse perspectives and collaborative problem-solving. Future generations of learners, equipped with cognitive enhancement methods that foster creativity, empathy, and critical thinking, are likely to innovate in ways that transcend traditional boundaries, promoting personal growth, societal change, and cognitive adaptability.

As we approach this future, ethical considerations underpinning memory and cognitive augmentation must remain at the forefront. Engaging in reflective dialogues about the implications of cognitive enhancements—balancing agency, privacy, and equity—will be essential as we redefine what it means to be intelligent in the digital age. Raising awareness around these discussions encourages individuals to be critical consumers of cognitive technologies, steering toward solutions that prioritize humane and inclusive cognitive development.

The potential for global collaboration in cognitive advancements is another compelling aspect of future cognition. As researchers, educators, and technologists from various fields engage across borders, knowledge-sharing initiatives can emerge that propel cognitive understanding to new heights. Collaborative research efforts aimed at exploring effective memory techniques across different cultural contexts can yield insights into universal principles of memory enhancement adaptable to disparate learning environments.

In anticipation of the future of evolution in cognition, it is vital to challenge existing educational paradigms and redefine what constitutes cognitive success. We must prioritize emotional intelligence, social skills, and creative problem-solving, embracing a holistic approach that values these attributes alongside traditional measures of intelligence. By fostering an educational framework that nurtures the entire spectrum of human potential, we can cultivate individuals prepared to thrive in an unpredictable and multifaceted world.

In conclusion, the future of cognition holds numerous possibilities driven by memory techniques, cognitive enhancements, and societal advancements. By embracing adaptive practices rooted in neuroscience and technology while fostering emotional and social intelligence, we can shape the trajectory of our cognitive evolution. As we embark on this journey toward understanding cognition's future, we remain committed to nurturing a rich tapestry of skills that celebrate personal growth and collective intelligence, empowering future generations to navigate the complexities of an ever-changing world.

- The Ever-Changing Landscape of Memory Content: The landscape of memory is an intricate tapestry woven from historical perspectives, contemporary understanding, and the evolving societal context in which we inhabit. As our grasp of memory continues to deepen, the recognition that memory is not a static construct but a dynamic process underscores its adaptability to societal changes, technological advancements, and individual needs. This exploration considers the multifaceted nature of memory, anticipating how it will evolve in response to emerging trends and challenges.

Historically, memory techniques have evolved alongside human society—rooted in the cultural practices of oral traditions and storytelling, moving through the ages to contemporary techniques centered on cognitive science and technology. Early methods of memorization were driven by the need for survival, as communities relied on passing down essential knowledge and skills through rich narratives. This intertwining of memory and culture captured diverse experiences and contexts, leading to a deeply rooted understanding of memory as both an individual and communal asset.

Building upon this historical foundation, the landscape of memory has experienced significant transformations with the advent of technology. The rise of digital tools—ranging from mobile applications to AI-driven learning platforms—has fundamentally altered the way individuals approach memory enhancement. Innovations that integrate memory techniques into interactive digital formats cater to modern learners, allowing them to engage with information in playful and meaningful ways. This shift toward technology-infused learning emphasizes that memory is not solely about retention but also about connectivity, creativity, and active engagement with the material.

In addition, the growing recognition of the importance of mental health and well-being significantly shapes the landscape of memory. Awareness of the impacts of stress, anxiety, and emotional states on memory function underscores the interplay between cognitive performance and psychological health. Educational approaches that prioritize emotional intelligence, mental well-being, and social support can foster a climate conducive to learning. As we recognize the essential role of emotions in memory retention, we can design strategies that integrate emotional awareness in both cognitive enhancement initiatives and educational frameworks.

Anticipating the future of memory, we must be vigilant to remain adaptable as societal contexts continue to transform. The future landscape of memory may be characterized by hybrid models that combine traditional techniques with innovative digital tools. The convergence of human cognition and machine intelligence presents myriad possibilities for enhancing memory, yet remains contingent on ethical considerations, responsible usage, and inclusivity. Collectively, we must navigate the landscape of memory with an emphasis on transparency, accessibility, and user agency, ensuring that advancements in memory enhancement benefit individuals from all walks of life.

Further, the future of memory may involve deeper insights into the neurological underpinnings of memory processes, driven by continued advancements in cognitive neuroscience. Researchers will likely explore the intricate interactions between various brain regions involved in memory consolidation, retrieval, and emotional processing. This knowledge may translate into targeted cognitive training interventions that enhance memory alongside understanding the unique needs of individuals at different life stages.

Cultural reflections on memory are crucial as well. The evolution of memory in context with historical experiences, societal values, and collective memory practices holds the potential to inform the design of memory techniques that resonate with diverse communities. By engaging with different cultural perspectives, we can expand our toolkit of memory strategies, ensuring that cognitive enhancements honor and respect the legacies of various communities.

In summary, the landscape of memory is ever-changing, evolving with the passage of time and the influence of technology, mental health awareness, and societal transformations. As we anticipate the future of memory, it is essential to cultivate adaptable practices that marry traditional techniques with innovative advancements while prioritizing emotional well-being, inclusivity, and cultural significance. Embracing the dynamic nature of memory points toward an enriching journey of discovery, personal growth, and cognitive empowerment—ultimately leading to a deeper understanding of our shared human experience.

15.5. The Future of International Cognitive Efforts

Memory and cognition have always been pivotal elements of human experience, and as we venture into the future, the landscape of memory enhancement will undoubtedly continue to evolve. The future of international cognitive efforts reveals a potential fusion of ancient wisdom with contemporary understanding and technology, a powerful promise that calls for collaboration among diverse champions of memory and learning.

To begin with, we must acknowledge that memory techniques are steeped in historical context and cultural significance. As we advance towards a future of cognitive enhancement, those engaged in memory efforts must remain committed to understanding and preserving the rich narratives that these techniques carry. By recognizing the diverse cultural practices surrounding memory across the globe, international cognitive efforts can benefit from a holistic approach that values the unique contributions of various societies. This inclusion will not only enhance the strategies used but also reinforce the sense of community in the shared quest for knowledge and memory mastery.

The role of technology in shaping the future of memory enhancement cannot be overstated. The integration of cutting-edge tools—such as artificial intelligence, virtual reality, and mobile applications—opens avenues for amplifying memory techniques. International collaborations can facilitate the sharing of research findings and technological innovations across borders, laying the groundwork for a global network dedicated to enhancing cognitive skills. By pooling resources and expertise, diverse teams can pioneer new platforms that capitalize on advancements in neuroscience and cognitive psychology, thereby revolutionizing the way memory techniques are applied in educational and professional settings.

One vital aspect of these collaborative efforts will involve establishing universal standards for cognitive enhancement practices. Governance surrounding memory techniques must prioritize ethics, accessibility, and inclusivity to ensure that advancements benefit all individuals, regardless of socioeconomic backgrounds. Developing global policies that recognize the rights of individuals, engage communities in the conversation, and promote equitable access to cognitive tools can create a solid foundation for collective growth. These policies can stimulate international discourse on the implications of cognitive enhancement—addressing concerns such as data privacy, consent, and the preservation of individual autonomy in the face of advanced technology.

Furthermore, global cognitive initiatives must embrace localized approaches that are culturally relevant and responsive to the unique needs of various populations. Memory techniques must be tailored to resonate with different communities' values, experiences, and educational systems. Collaborative research can uncover the cultural nuances of memory perception and encoding strategies, enabling a nuanced understanding of how cognitive approaches can be adapted effectively within diverse contexts. By ensuring that cognitive enhancement practices honor and adapt to cultural identities, international cognitive efforts can create a broader and more inclusive definition of memory enhancement that honors the complexity of human cognition.

In addition, fostering multi-disciplinary collaboration across fields such as psychology, education, neuroscience, and technology will drive innovation in memory enhancement. Creating platforms for communication and dialogue among researchers, practitioners, educators, and policymakers can facilitate meaningful partnerships that harness collective knowledge. By working together to translate theoretical insights into practical memory strategies, these collaborations will yield effective initiatives that resonate with learners at every stage of life.

As we consider educational opportunities on an international scale, it is vital to initiate programs that prioritize cognitive skills from an early age. Targeting educational reforms that incorporate memory enhancement techniques—be it through interactive apps, memory palaces, or gamified learning—can empower the next generation to navigate an increasingly complex information landscape. Creating a global movement to share best practices in memory education can transcend borders, ensuring that children everywhere have access to memory-enhancing resources.

Finally, reflecting on the implications of the ongoing journey towards international cognitive efforts, we must recognize that the future of memory enhancement is not just an isolated pursuit—it is an embodiment of our shared human experience. By fostering opportunities for collaboration, dialogue, and mutual support, we cultivate a community united by the understanding that memory is a vital part of identity, learning, and connection.

In summary, the future of international cognitive efforts presents boundless possibilities, enriched by a spirit of collaboration and respect for the cultural significance of memory. By effectively intertwining ancient wisdom with innovative approaches, emphasizing accessibility, inclusive policymaking, and cross-disciplinary engagement, the global community can embark on a transformative journey that enhances memory and cognition for all. As we unite our strengths, we pave the way for a future where cognitive enhancement is celebrated, shared, and sustained, unlocking extraordinary potential within humanity.

16. The Science of Remembering: An Evolutionary Perspective

16.1. Memory in Primitive Societies

Memory in primitive societies provides a fascinating window into how early humans utilized cognitive processes for survival and social cohesion. In these communities, memory was not merely a function of retaining facts but an essential mechanism for navigating their environments, preserving cultural knowledge, and ensuring the continuity of their social fabric. This exploratory narrative highlights the critical role of memory in primitive societies, focusing on their methods, techniques, and the implications of memory enhancement within the historical context of human cognition.

In primitive societies, the survival of individuals and groups hinged on their ability to encode and recall essential information about their surroundings, food sources, social relationships, and ecological changes. Early humans did not have the written language as a means to document their histories; thus, memory techniques stemmed largely from oral traditions—largely dependent on storytelling and shared experiences. The practice of passing down knowledge through stories embodied not just entertainment but a pivotal method for encoding crucial survival skills and cultural wisdom. These narratives often incorporated vivid imagery and emotional resonance, allowing for deeper encoding of the information and heightened recall.

Key techniques in memory preservation revolved around mnemonic devices intimately tied to communal experiences. Storytelling, for instance, was a potent mnemonic tool that enabled individuals to learn and remember intricate details about their environment. Stories embedded with lessons regarding hunting, gathering, and seasonal patterns became integral to the community's collective memory. By embedding knowledge within a narrative context, early humans enriched their recollections, ensuring that vital information persisted through generations.

Spatial memory also played a crucial role in the survival of primitive societies. Individuals learned the geography of their surroundings, identifying landmarks, resource locations, and migration routes with precision. Memory of spatial layouts acted as a cognitive map, enabling early humans to navigate vast territories without written maps. This capability provided an evolutionary advantage, positioning those with superior spatial memory skills to locate food sources, evade predators, and engage more effectively in social interactions—a fundamental component of community survival.

As social structures evolved, the intricacies of memory within primitive societies were further developed. Individuals relied heavily on memory to navigate interpersonal relationships, embodying social norms and identifying allies or threats. Memory allowed for the recall of past interactions, helping to build trust and community cohesion. The ability to remember individuals and their roles within the social group increased the success of collaborative endeavors, reinforcing alliances and minimizing conflict—practical adaptations critical for survival.

Adaptation through memory also reflects the cognitive evolution occurring within these primitive societies. Memory is inherently layered and complex; as early humans faced new challenges, their cognitive capabilities expanded to encompass not just survival but social development as well. The need to retain nuanced details about their environment and interpersonal relations led to the evolution of increasingly sophisticated cognitive strategies, enhancing problem-solving skills as communities grew and became more interconnected.

The integration of memory practices into social and cultural norms created a rich landscape where knowledge was not only preserved but celebrated. Rituals and communal gatherings served as platforms for reinforcing memory by inviting collective participation in storytelling, shared discovery, and emotional engagement. These practices cultivated social bonds that transcended individual experiences, weaving together the fabric of collective memory.

In conclusion, memory in primitive societies served as a foundational element essential for survival, social cohesion, and cultural continuity. The techniques and practices evolved not merely as tools for information storage but as vital components of human existence, guiding early humans in navigating their world. Exploring the significance of memory within this context offers invaluable insights into the origins of cognitive enhancement practices, illustrating how the adaptive nature of memory informed human development and paved the way for the complexities of cognition we explore today.

16.2. Evolutionary Necessity: Why We Remember

Memory serves as one of the most intricate and dynamic functions of the human brain, encompassing a series of complex processes that allow us to encode, store, and retrieve information. To grasp the essence of memory at the physiological level, one must delve into the neural underpinnings that orchestrate this multifaceted phenomenon. At its core, memory formation involves neurons—specialized cells that transmit electrical signals throughout the brain and body. These neurons are the fundamental building blocks of the nervous system, and their active communication is vital for all cognitive functions, particularly memory.

Memory can be broadly categorized into different types, the most fundamental being explicit (declarative) memory and implicit (non-declarative) memory. Explicit memory can be further divided into episodic memory, which pertains to personal experiences and specific events, and semantic memory, which relates to facts and general knowledge. Implicit memory encompasses skills and conditioned responses developed through practice or repetition. Understanding how these types of memory are processed requires a closer look at what happens in the brain during memory formation.

Encoding—an essential stage of memory processing—occurs when sensory information is transformed into a form that can be stored. The hippocampus, located within the temporal lobe, plays a crucial role in this phase. It acts as a gateway for new information, facilitating the transition from short-term memory to long-term memory. During encoding, the hippocampus interacts with various regions of the brain, including sensory areas and prefrontal regions, which contribute to higher-order cognitive functions such as attention and working memory. This interplay ensures that information is associated with relevant sensory experiences and contextual cues, enhancing the likelihood of successful retrieval later on.

Once encoded, information is consolidated, a process that transforms fragile short-term memories into more stable long-term memories. Consolidation primarily occurs during sleep and involves the strengthening of neural connections known as synapses. Repeated activation of specific neural pathways leads to structural changes in the brain, reinforcing synaptic connections—a phenomenon known as synaptic plasticity. The mechanisms of synaptic plasticity are heavily influenced by neurotransmitters, such as glutamate, which facilitate communication between neurons. Repeated activation results in long-lasting changes, commonly referred to as long-term potentiation (LTP), which plays a fundamental role in learning and memory.

The retrieval of memories—the process through which stored information is accessed—depends heavily on the cues present at the time of recall. This is where the associative nature of memory comes into play. The brain utilizes various cues, such as sensory inputs or contextual information, to trigger the activation of neural networks associated with a specific memory. Regions such as the cortex, which contain consolidated memories, work in tandem with the hippocampus to facilitate this retrieval process. Moreover, the emotional significance attached to certain memories, often processed by the amygdala, can enhance retrieval efficiency. Emotionally charged memories tend to be more vivid and easier to recall, shedding light on the interplay between emotion and memory.

Neurotransmitters also play a significant role in memory processes. Apart from glutamate, other neurotransmitters such as dopamine and acetylcholine are crucial for modulating memory functions. Dopamine is particularly important when it comes to reward-based learning; it reinforces the connections between neurons when an action leads to a positive outcome, thus enhancing the encoding of those memories. Acetylcholine, meanwhile, is linked to attention and arousal, supporting the encoding of new memories and facilitating memory retrieval.

As we investigate the neural foundations of memory, it is also pertinent to recognize that memory is not static; it is adaptive and malleable. The concept of neuroplasticity—the brain's ability to reorganize itself functionally and structurally in response to learning and experience—plays an essential role here. Neuroplasticity allows for the formation of new neural connections, the rearrangement of existing pathways, and the ability to recover from injuries. In the context of memory, this means that experiences can refine and reshape our memory systems, enabling us to learn more effectively and to adapt to new environments.

Furthermore, the brain's capacity for neuroplasticity can be harnessed through deliberate practice and mnemonic techniques, including those explored in the realm of memory palaces. By creating structured environments in the mind, individuals can facilitate the encoding and retrieval of information in a more organized and effective manner. Thus, memory palaces not only serve as vivid mnemonic aids but also take advantage of the brain's inherent adaptability, promoting an enduring capacity for memory enhancement.

In conclusion, exploring the neural foundations of memory reveals the intricate and interconnected processes that underpin how we learn, remember, and recall. Memory is not merely a passive archive of experiences; it is a dynamic interplay of various brain regions, neurotransmitters, and synaptic activities, all supported by the overarching phenomena of neuroplasticity. As our understanding of memory at the physiological level deepens, the implications for cognitive enhancement strategies grow clearer. Techniques such as memory palaces actively engage these neural mechanisms, allowing individuals to leverage their brain's natural capabilities for improved memory performance, ultimately transforming how we approach learning and retention in an increasingly complex world.

16.3. Adaptive Memory Theory

Adaptive Memory Theory presents a compelling framework for understanding the intricate dynamics of memory as it evolves alongside human survival and cognitive needs. At its core, the theory posits that human memory is not merely a static repository of information; rather, it has been shaped by evolutionary pressures to enhance adaptability, allowing individuals to thrive in various environments and contexts. Memory, in this sense, has a functional focus that transcends rote retention, adapting to serve the demands of changing circumstances and the complexities of human experiences.

One of the pivotal aspects of Adaptive Memory Theory is the recognition of the selective nature of what we remember. Research has shown that memory is often biased toward information that is deemed relevant to survival, social interactions, and emotional significance. This selectivity aligns with the idea that memory systems have evolved to prioritize encoding information that enhances our chances of survival and reproductive success. For instance, early humans who remembered critical details about food sources, predator behaviors, or social alliances were better positioned to navigate their environments effectively. Such memories provided immediate benefits and fostered adaptability, a key component of evolutionary fitness.

In contemporary contexts, the principles of Adaptive Memory Theory offer a lens through which to view the applicability of memory techniques in our daily lives. The information overload characteristic of the digital age presents unique challenges to memory and cognition. As individuals face incessant streams of data, the mechanisms of memory must adapt to filter and prioritize what is deemed essential. Memory technologies and enhancement techniques, such as mnemonic devices, can be seen as tools that support this adaptation by creating structures for efficient information processing and retrieval. The design of memory aids—like memory palaces—allows individuals to anchor abstract concepts within a spatial framework, facilitating recall through contextual associations.

Moreover, the impact of emotional and contextual cues on memory retrieval underscores the adaptive function of memory. Emotionally charged experiences are more likely to be retained, making them significant for creating lasting memories that inform future behaviors. In navigating complex social environments, the ability to remember individuals, their relationships, and key interactions is paramount. This emotional engagement builds a framework for understanding social dynamics and aids in the formation of connections crucial for survival and collaboration. By employing adaptive strategies that leverage emotional relevance—such as associating information with personal experiences—individuals can enhance both retention and applicability of knowledge.

As we look toward the future of cognitive enhancement, one can predict the evolution of memory through the increasing integration of technology. The rise of artificial intelligence, machine learning, and cognitive training applications has the potential to revolutionize the way we engage with memory processes. By harnessing adaptive algorithms that analyze learning behaviors and cognitive patterns, technology can facilitate personalized learning experiences that cater to individual memory needs. This evolution heralds a new era where cognitive enhancement becomes entwined with our daily lives, fostering resilience, creativity, and adaptability.

However, this forward trajectory must be met with consideration for ethical implications and societal impacts. As we embrace the opportunities presented by emerging cognitive enhancement technologies, we must also grapple with questions of equity, privacy, and the authenticity of our cognitive experiences. There is a responsibility to ensure that access to cognitive enhancement resources is equitable, fostering a landscape where individuals from all backgrounds can benefit from advancements in memory and cognitive training.

In conclusion, Adaptive Memory Theory offers a robust framework for understanding the evolutionary purpose of memory as it adapts to meet our cognitive needs. By recognizing the selective nature of memory, we can appreciate the significance of techniques that enhance information retention in a rapidly changing world. As we navigate the future of cognitive enhancement, the interplay between memory, emotional engagement, and technology provides fertile ground for innovation. Embracing the principles of adaptation encourages us to harvest the potential of our cognitive abilities, ultimately empowering individuals to thrive in an increasingly complex and interconnected society.

16.4. The Future of Evolution in Cognition

The concept of the future of evolution in cognition is intrinsically linked to our rapidly changing environment, technological advancements, and the increasing demands placed on the human brain as we adapt to new challenges. As we stand on the brink of significant breakthroughs in neuroscience, artificial intelligence, and cognitive enhancement methods, it becomes imperative to consider how our cognitive functions, particularly memory, will evolve to accommodate these changes.

One of the most pivotal aspects of this evolution is the potential for enhanced memory capacity through integration with digital technologies. The rise of smart devices and applications that support memory retention through spaced repetition, gamification, and visualization techniques illustrates a shift in how we engage with information. These tools are poised to transform traditional educational paradigms, making learning more collaborative and interactive, ultimately reshaping cognitive processes. As we become increasingly reliant on technology for memory support, our cognitive architecture may adapt, leading to new modes of remembering and recalling information that blend human capacity with machine efficiency.

Moreover, as cognitive demands rise in the face of globalization and an explosion of information, the brain's ability to filter, prioritize, and retrieve relevant knowledge will be crucial. Evolution has equipped our brains with remarkable flexibility and neuroplasticity; however, the contemporary pace of change may push these boundaries. Future cognitive strategies may necessitate a deeper understanding of how memory functions in the digital age, where information is ubiquitous and real-time decision-making is vital. This context points towards a potential evolution of memory from passive retention to active engagement, where individuals adaptively harness technology to enhance their cognitive capabilities.

The increasing importance of emotional intelligence in professional and personal contexts also indicates a shift in the evolutionary trajectory of cognition. Research continues to demonstrate that emotional connections significantly enhance memory retention and recall. Consequently, approaches to memory enhancement may need to focus more on integrating emotional contexts into cognitive frameworks. Future cognitive enhancement techniques may prioritize narrative-based memory strategies, allowing individuals to forge deeper emotional ties with the material they are learning, thereby facilitating greater retention.

Furthermore, societal implications of enhanced cognition will necessitate a reevaluation of our understanding of intelligence itself. As cognitive enhancement technologies democratize access to knowledge, the defining traits of intelligence may evolve from traditional academic achievements to encompass emotional, creative, and critical thinking abilities. This shift emphasizes the significance of creativity and adaptability as integral components of intelligence in modern and future contexts.

However, as we anticipate these revolutionary changes, ethical considerations surrounding the use of cognitive enhancements become increasingly pressing. The line between enhancement and manipulation must be carefully examined, and a dialogue must be established about the implications of altering cognitive processes. Ensuring equitable access to cognitive enhancement tools is paramount; as advancements unfold, it is crucial that marginalized populations are not left behind. Inclusive strategies must guide the implementation of cognitive enhancement technologies, ensuring that individual agency, privacy, and consent are prioritized.

Finally, culture plays an undeniably pivotal role in shaping our approaches to memory and cognition. As our world becomes more interconnected, the cross-pollination of cultural practices around memory will inform our understanding of cognitive strategies. Diverse insights can lead to enriched memory techniques that resonate with individuals from various backgrounds, resulting in more holistic approaches to cognitive enhancement.

In summary, the future of evolution in cognition promises to be an exciting journey characterized by the integration of technology, an emphasis on emotional intelligence, shifting definitions of intelligence, and the ethical considerations that accompany these advancements. By grappling with these dynamics, society can position itself for a future where cognitive enhancement serves to empower individuals, enrich their learning experiences, and foster resilience in an ever-evolving world. Ultimately, this evolution holds immense potential to redefine the landscape of memory and intelligence for generations to come, creating a rich tapestry of cognitive growth that celebrates the best of human potential.

16.5. The Ever-Changing Landscape of Memory

The landscape of memory is one that is continuously evolving, shaped by advancements in technology, changes in societal needs, and our growing understanding of cognitive processes. As we explore the dynamic nature of memory, it becomes evident that its evolution is influenced by several factors ranging from cultural practices to neuropsychological research, all of which contribute to how we enhance, retain, and utilize memory in our lives.

Historically, memory techniques have been fundamental to cultural identity and knowledge preservation. In primitive societies, for instance, memory was critical for survival, used to pass down essential information about hunting strategies, foraging locations, and social hierarchies. As societies progressed, so did our memory strategies, evolving from oral traditions of storytelling to more structured mnemonic techniques—a transition exemplified by the development of the Method of Loci. These historical foundations highlight that memory has always served to connect individuals to their environments, communities, and cultures, laying the groundwork for how we interact with knowledge today.

In modern society, the advent of digital technology has further transformed the landscape of memory. With unprecedented access to information through the internet, social media, and various digital tools, individuals are now faced with both an abundance of resources and the challenge of information overload. In this context, the ability to retain and retrieve relevant information becomes critical. Memory techniques, particularly innovative applications of traditional methods—such as digital memory palaces and spaced repetition—are becoming more widespread, driven by the need to adapt to this rapidly changing informational landscape.

Moreover, research in cognitive neuroscience reveals that our understanding of memory is continuously evolving. Studies have shown that memory is not a singular function of the brain but rather a complex interplay of different brain regions working collaboratively to encode, consolidate, and retrieve information. As we learn more about these processes, particularly the role of neuroplasticity in memory formation and retention, we realize the implications for how we can enhance memory through intentional practices and techniques.

The fusion of memory enhancement techniques with advancements in artificial intelligence presents exciting possibilities for the future. AI-powered learning tools that analyze individual memory patterns and preferences can offer personalized strategies for cognitive enhancement. By tailoring techniques to individual learning styles, we open the door to a more tailored approach to memory training, ensuring that cognitive enhancement becomes more effective and accessible for diverse groups.

The emphasis on emotional intelligence and its connection to memory further underscores the importance of a holistic understanding of cognition. Emotional experiences are often more memorable than neutral events, reinforcing the idea that memory is not solely a cognitive function but also involves emotional engagement and social dynamics. Therefore, future memory enhancement approaches may increasingly integrate emotional and social factors, fostering stronger connections between learners and the material.

Societal implications of memory enhancement also merit consideration. As cognitive augmentation becomes more normalized in various contexts—from educational institutions to workplaces—questions regarding equitable access to these techniques arise. The risk of creating a cognitive divide based on socioeconomic status, education level, or geographical location should not be overlooked. Ensuring that all individuals can benefit from advancements in memory enhancement technology will be crucial in fostering an inclusive society that values cognitive development across socio-economic spectra.

As we contemplate the future of memory, the interplay of global perspectives must also be acknowledged. The rise of global exchanges of knowledge allows for the sharing of diverse memory strategies and cognitive approaches rooted in different cultures. This privilege of cross-cultural dialogue enriches our understanding of memory and can lead to a more comprehensive suite of memory enhancement techniques that can be adopted universally.

In conclusion, the ever-changing landscape of memory is characterized by its adaptability, evolving practices, and the profound interplay between culture, technology, and cognitive science. By recognizing the importance of memory as both a personal and communal asset, we lay the groundwork for innovative approaches that empower individuals to optimize their cognitive capabilities. As we navigate this complexity, a commitment to ethical engagement, equity, and inclusiveness will be essential to ensuring that memory enhancement serves as a tool for personal growth and collective advancement. Moving forward, we should celebrate the innate potential of memory and its integral role in shaping human experience as we envision a future where cognition thrives, innovation flourishes, and memory remains a bridge connecting us to our past, present, and future.

9798315468912